The Inclusion Equation

The Inclusion Equation

Leveraging Data & AI for Organizational Diversity and Well-being

Dr. Serena H. Huang

FIRST EDITION

WILEY

Published by John Wiley & Sons, Inc., Hoboken, New Jersey.
Published simultaneously in Canada.

For general information on our other products and services or for technical support, please contact our Customer Care Department within the United States at (800) 762-2974, outside the United States at (317) 572-3993 or fax (317) 572-4002.

Wiley also publishes its books in a variety of electronic formats. Some content that appears in print may not be available in electronic formats. For more information about Wiley products, visit our web site at www.wiley.com.

Library of Congress Cataloging-in-Publication Data has been applied for:

Paperback ISBN: 9781394294510
ePDF ISBN: 9781394294534
ePUB ISBN: 9781394294527

Cover Images: Artificial intelligence set of web icons in line style. AI technology icons for web and mobile app. Machine learning, digital AI technology, algorithm, smart robotic and cloud computing network. © Misha Shutkevych/Getty ImagesHeart nature design vector. © 123456/Getty ImagesPuzzles icons set. Puzzle pieces, parts, linear icon collection. Line with editable stroke. © Matsabe/Getty Images
Cover Design: Wiley

Set in STIXTwoText by Lumina Datamatics

SKY10093894_121924

Contents

About the Author

Dr. Serena Huang is revolutionizing how organizations approach talent, well-being, and DEI through data and AI. As a people analytics executive and chief data officer, Dr. Huang spent more than a decade leading measurement and analytics strategy for DEI and ESG at iconic brands like GE, Kraft Heinz, and PayPal.

A highly sought-after international speaker and one of the 2024 Top AI Keynote Speakers, Dr. Huang's insightful keynotes and practical workshops have reached leaders across Asia, North America, and Europe. She also energizes the next generation as a guest lecturer at top MBA programs, including Wharton, Haas, and Kellogg.

In 2023, LinkedIn Learning recruited Dr. Huang to develop one of their most popular online courses on using data to drive meaningful progress in DEI and employee well-being. She was also invited to keynote the National Alliance on Mental Illness annual conference on effective workplace mental health strategies.

Dr. Huang recently founded *Data with Serena* to empower people and organizations through data and AI. Through strategic advisory services, she is helping businesses worldwide actualize a new vision of work where employee well-being and belonging are prioritized alongside profits.

When not traveling, Serena recharges through running, golf, and creating wellness content for her YouTube channel.

Acknowledgments

As I reflect on the journey of writing *The Inclusion Equation*, I am filled with gratitude for all the individuals who have supported, inspired, and encouraged me along the way.

First and foremost, I want to express my deepest gratitude to my family, who have been my rock throughout this journey. To my parents, Frank, Helen, Conni, and Tom I thank you for instilling in me the values of hard work, perseverance, and compassion. Your guidance and wisdom have shaped me into the person I am today, and I am forever grateful. To my aunt, Sophie, I am grateful for your encouragement since Day 1. To my husband, Naty, I thank you for your unwavering support and patience.

I also want to acknowledge the incredible friends who have been a part of my journey. To Mike Pino, Welu Aningo, Sonny Rivera, Lisa Lee, Karen Eber, Spencer Nicholls, Leonard Green, Holly Lam, Theresia Kurnia, Bas Debbink, Sophia Toh, and Jenny Dunten, I thank you for your friendship, encouragement, and support. Your presence in my life has made a significant impact, and I cherish our relationships.

I had my moment of "I am on the right track" when I started interviewing practitioners and this book would not have been the practical guide I wanted it to be without their experience and insights. A heartfelt thank you to Dawn Klinghoffer, Dr. Alexis Fink, Dr. Stephanie Murphy, Dr. Sanja Licina, Chris Cummings, Shujaat Ahmad, César Lostaunau, Carlo Dela Fuente, Tashi Theisman, Cindi Howson, Dan Riley, and Lani Hall for contributing to *The Inclusion Equation*.

Throughout my career, I have been fortunate to have had the opportunity to work with and learn from some of the most talented and dedicated individuals in the field of people analytics, DEI, and well-being. To my colleagues, mentors, and peers, I thank you for your expertise, guidance, and collaboration. Your contributions to this field have been invaluable, and I am honored to have had the chance to learn from and work alongside you.

A special thank you goes to Lani Hall, who is the first chief diversity and inclusion officer and HR leader I've met who not only believed in data but believed in me. I wouldn't have started the data analytics work on DEI if it weren't for her willingness to push the envelope when we worked together at GE.

I would also like to acknowledge the numerous individuals who have inspired me through their work, writing, and advocacy. To Dr. Fei-Fei Li, I thank you for your thought-provoking writing and research in "The Words I See." Writing a book isn't easy. Elaine Lin Hering generously provided timely advice that kept me going at a very critical moment. Her work on "Unlearning Silence" also serves as a constant reminder when I think about the important message I want to share with the world.

In writing *The Inclusion Equation*, I have been driven by a passion to create a more inclusive and equitable world. I hope that this book will inspire and empower others to join me on this journey, and I am grateful for the opportunity to share my thoughts and ideas with a wider audience.

Thank you again to everyone who has supported me on this journey. I am honored to have had the chance to share my work with you.

Introduction

There is no well-being without inclusion.

– Dr. Serena Huang

The phone rang close to midnight—an unknown number I almost ignored. But something made me answer.

"Hi Serena, it's Sara...," The voice on the other end was shaky, laced with confusion and fear.

"Hello...Sara? Are you okay?"

"I...I woke up in the ER. I don't know what happened...."

My heart sank as she apologized profusely about a work deadline she might miss, her biggest concern mere hours after a medical crisis. Sara didn't report to me directly and was working on a project of mine as a cross-functional stretch assignment.

In that moment, a thousand worries flooded my mind. Had I been so demanding as a leader that she felt compelled to call about work deliverables from a hospital bed? Why didn't I notice the signs that she was struggling on weekly project team calls?

I assured her that her health was the priority—not the project, not the deadlines. Anything else could wait.

There was a long pause before Sara's voice cracked again. "Can I...can I ask you something?" I could hear her trepidation.

"Anything, Sara," I reassured her.

"The doctor said I had a panic attack...,"she said, her voice barely above a whisper. "I didn't even know what they were. They said I've been having them for a while. What should I do?"

My stomach tightened. This wasn't just a personal struggle; it was a symptom of a broken system. Sara, a talented employee, was suffering in silence, afraid to seek help.

"Sara, you're not alone," I said, my voice firming. "Our company has an employee assistance program (EAP)—free confidential counseling. You can talk to licensed professionals and get help there."

"My manager wouldn't find out?" she asked, her voice laced with fear.

"It's confidential, Sara," I assured her. "Your privacy is protected."

That call was a turning point. It wasn't just about Sara; it was about countless others struggling in silence. Sara was the first, but unfortunately not the last, Asian woman who would call me asking for help with a similar challenge at work over the years.

It ignited a fire within me, a burning desire to break the stigma around mental health at work. I started researching, delving into the disparities in access to mental healthcare for BIPOC (Black, Indigenous, and people of color) communities. The stories I uncovered were heartbreaking, highlighting the urgent need for change.

The Problem

After realizing how stigma holds employees back from seeking help and the unique challenges faced by individuals from different backgrounds, I began to wonder why employee well-being and diversity, equity, and inclusion (DEI) are often treated as separate initiatives within organizations.

Traditionally, corporate well-being programs focus on stress management, mental health resources, and work-life balance. Often benefits become the only solution an employer can provide to address these issues. DEI initiatives, on the other hand, address issues of representation, bias, and inclusion. Rather than benefits, various initiatives and programs are created to improve the hiring, development, and retention of employees from diverse backgrounds. Both well-being and DEI impact an employee's experience at work. This siloed approach fails to recognize the interconnected nature of these two areas.

A truly inclusive and equitable workplace cannot exist without prioritizing employee well-being. Employees from marginalized groups often face unique barriers to accessing support due to stigma, fear of judgment, or lack of culturally sensitive resources. This can lead to underutilization of healthcare services, hindering individual and organizational growth. Furthermore, the experiences of individuals are shaped by the intersection of multiple identities. A Black woman, for example, may face unique challenges related to both race and gender, requiring tailored support and interventions. Veterans transitioning from military into their first civilian jobs, on the other hand, may experience drastically different issues. Because demographic and life experiences create different challenges, treating DEI and well-being as separate programs fails to address this complex reality.

Historical Context and Evolution

The year 2020 hit all of us in different ways. The COVID-19 pandemic and the death of George Floyd brought concerns about DEI, health, and well-being to the forefront.

I remember it was nearly impossible to have conversations about measuring health and well-being at work prior to the pandemic. I started reading about how different organizations would go beyond employee engagement and measure their employees' well-being in regular surveys back in 2019. When I spoke about the topic at the time, very few organizations were capturing this data in the employee engagement survey. Fast forward to March 2020, the moment the world went into lockdown, the C-suite leadership team reached out asking who could help provide real-time data on the health and well-being of employees. I was the global head of people analytics at one of the largest food companies in the world at the time. Remember when canned food would fly off the shelf in the grocery store? The health of our employees suddenly became critical to the global supply chain of food. Overnight, they became frontline workers. My team ended up creating a COVID-19 dashboard for the senior leadership team, which included both internal and external data by location. We also launched the company's first-ever health and well-being survey to better understand how to provide the right level of support. We noticed that mental health was an area many employees needed help with and that parents with young children were also having a difficult time. It was some of the most challenging, emotionally taxing yet rewarding work I've done in my career. My team ended up reaching an award from the CEO for being "data heroes" in the pandemic.

As companies navigate this post-pandemic world, it's crucial for businesses to prioritize creating an inclusive and healthy environment for employees. When employees feel seen and valued, they're more productive and likely to stay with the company long term. In fact, a study by McKinsey found that companies with diverse workforces are 35% more likely to outperform their less diverse peers. On the other hand, the cost of not prioritizing inclusion and well-being can be staggering. A study by the World Health Organization (WHO) found that depression and anxiety disorders cost the global economy more than $1 trillion in lost productivity annually.

The Business Case for Prioritizing DEI and Well-being

There has been a business case for inclusion for quite some time. But after the 2020 protests after the deaths of George Floyd, Breonna Taylor, and Ahmaud Arbery, along with the many Asian hate tragedies, there was a new focus on inequities and injustice leading to a *new* business case for inclusion. Companies could no longer wait for external or internal situations to spark change. In parallel, the isolation during lockdown, along with the grief of losing family and friends due to COVID-19, made it more acceptable to open up about not feeling okay. Everyone suddenly had a shared experience of being away from loved ones and having to work in drastically different ways.

Can you be productive when you are unwell? Whether it's a physical issue or an emotional one, you are not operating at 100% when you aren't feeling 100%. However, stigma holds us back from talking about mental health at work and seeking the help we need.

I recall seeing one social media post from Adam Grant that went viral, and it said, "It's okay to call in sick. It's also okay to call in sad." What a timely reminder. Have you ever needed a mental health day before the pandemic when it was not as acceptable to say out loud? Are you working in an environment where mental health benefits are offered but taboo to talk about?

In my conversations, I've heard some executives put discrete personal appointments on their calendar while others openly label their regular therapy sessions to ensure they were protected. There isn't a right or wrong approach, but the underlying reason for why someone would worry about sharing they are in therapy is worth examining. Some of us have run into managers who are not as understanding of mental health needs, and we naturally want to protect our career. Certain cultures also have open discussions about mental health. Understanding the reason why employees hide their needs can be very helpful to creating programs to address the underlying issues.

Just because the COVID-19 pandemic is over doesn't mean employees no longer need support. In fact, many employees have continued to need help because of numerous factors that are out of their control, including high inflation and global conflicts. In a recent workshop, I facilitated a debate on who should be responsible for an employee's mental health. Is it the employees or their manager? The easy answer is both, of course. The manager and employee themselves need to both do their parts. By asking the group to take sides, it forces everyone to think more critically. One side of the room passionately argued that the employer and managers have a responsibility to keep their employees healthy mentally because managers have as much impact on our mental health as a significant other. The other side of the room articulated numerous reasons why managers should not be held responsible for things outside of work or beyond their control, such as illness in the family.

It's no secret that poor mental health impacts our lives, but many don't realize how it can also affect our businesses. According to the WHO, an estimated 15% of working-age adults have a mental disorder at any point in time. Depression and anxiety are estimated to cost the global economy US $1 trillion each year, driven predominantly by lost productivity. People living with severe mental health conditions are largely excluded from work despite participation in economic activities being important for recovery.

As reported by the American Psychiatric Association Foundation Center for Workplace Mental Health, employees with depression miss an average of 31.4 workdays each year and lose another 27.9 workdays to unproductivity—or presenteeism—which costs employers an estimated $44 billion annually.

Anxiety and chronic stress can also prevent employees from fully "showing up" to work, leading to reduced effectiveness and costly mistakes. In addition to impacting engagement and productivity, mental health issues can affect our creative efforts and ability to make decisions and solve problems.

Given the high prevalence of mental health conditions globally, your organization is bound to employ people who could benefit from your help.

What about the other employees who do not have mental health conditions? Is there a business case for improving their health and well-being?

Gallup researchers reviewed 736 studies across 347 organizations in 53 industries, with employees in 90 countries. Within each study, they statistically calculated the business-level relationship between employee engagement and business outcomes such as profitability and absenteeism. In total, they studied 183,806 business and work units that included 3,354,784 employees. Comparing top-quartile with bottom-quartile employee engagement, business/work units resulted in the following median percentage differences:

- Profitability: 23%
- Productivity (sales): 17%
- Turnover: 21% to 51%
- Safety incidents (accidents): 63%
- Absenteeism: 78%
- Patient safety incidents (mortality and falls): 58%

Is employee engagement the same as well-being? No, but the two measures are highly correlated in the studies.

The Interconnectedness of DEI and Well-being

It's easy to think that the DEI movement is losing steam. Social media is filled with anti-DEI sentiments and some US states have even defunded DEI programs. However, a survey of 600 C-Suite leaders of companies with more than 500 employees in 2024 shows 80% remain committed to DEI.[1]

Some organizations have created new names for DEI functions or combine talent with DEI into one. Inclusion goes far beyond being invited to meetings or team happy hours. It is also being included and having a voice in decisions that impact them.

Plus, the more research I read on employee well-being and mental health, the more obvious is the tight connection between DEI and well-being in the workplace.

Imagine the last time you felt excluded or left out of an important discussion at work. How did that impact your well-being? You likely felt a bit anxious and stressed, wondering why you were not part of the conversation.

Now, imagine having to avoid talking about your family because you weren't sure how accepting your colleagues would be of your nontraditional setup. Perhaps you are part of the LGBTQ community. Perhaps you have a blended family with stepchildren. Perhaps you are a single parent to adopted children. Perhaps you chose not to have children because of a rare genetic disorder that runs in your family. These are all valid reasons not to share or to cover your identity to avoid unwanted conversations.

Did you know more than 60% of employees engage in covering part of their identity in the workplace? People cover because they want to be included and feel like they belong, and they fear part of their identity prevents them from being accepted. It is not difficult to imagine the negative impact of constant covering on health and well-being.

One essential dimension of workplace well-being is "connection & community" according to the latest framework released by the US Surgeon General's *Framework for Workplace Mental Health and Well-being*. Research indicates that feelings of loneliness and inadequate emotional support significantly correlate with a heightened risk of self-harm and suicidal ideation.[2] Additionally, insufficient social connections are linked to an elevated risk of various health issues, including a 29% increased likelihood of heart disease and a 32% increased risk of stroke.[3]

Additionally, demographic background plays a significant role in mental health. The analysis from CARE International shows that 27% of women experienced increased mental health struggles due to COVID-19, compared with 10% of men.[4] Reports from Columbia

University suggest that a Black adult is 20% more likely to experience a serious mental health concern than a White adult.[5]

The Solution: AI and Data Analytics

Despite the headlines of backlash on DEI, many organizations are just as committed to their DEI priorities as ever. However, there's a growing expectation that DEI initiatives must demonstrate a positive return on investment (ROI). This is where data and AI come into play.

We cannot improve what we don't measure. Measuring diversity is one thing, but quantifying inclusion is far more complex. Until recently, organizations have struggled to clearly quantify the level of inclusion because inclusion is a multifaceted concept. One common theme I've noticed in the leaders I've interviewed for this book is their focus on demonstrating business impact of DEI and well-being initiatives. Whether it's the impact of employee resource groups (ERGs) on hiring or promotions or the healthcare cost reduction from implementing specific well-being programs, those who are successful in securing more funding, run their programs like a business. They don't only focus on attendance for events or participation in programs, but instead, ask the tough questions of what business metric will this program improve and did we achieve that. These leaders either partner with analytics teams internally or external vendors to ensure the metrics are captured on day one.

The advancements in data analysis and AI technology have changed the game for measuring what previously seemed unmeasurable. The AI revolution, sparked by innovations like ChatGPT, has opened up new possibilities for measuring inclusion. By analyzing large amounts of text data from employee surveys, Slack conversations, and other sources, organizations can now gain a deeper understanding of their inclusion dynamics. The question on leaders' mind is no longer "What can we do?" but "What can't we do?"

Imagine a workplace where you receive personalized notifications reminding you to connect with a colleague you haven't spoken to in a while. Or where your calendar suggests alternative meeting times to be mindful of the schedules of your team members in a different time zone. This isn't the future—it's already here.

In a 2022 article, researchers at Stanford found that hundreds of firms are using AI to improve inclusion and belonging in the workplace.[6] Data analytics tools, which account for 32.3% of the tools in the study, collect real-time information on employee connections, inclusion, engagement, and sentiment. These tools use surveys, pulse checks, and communication metadata to assess belonging. Some tools also leverage sentiment analysis, network mapping, and internal reviews to provide a more comprehensive understanding of employee experiences. Additionally, behavior-change tools, which account for 26.5% of the tools in the study, use digital nudges to encourage inclusive behavior, provide feedback on learning and development opportunities, and offer actionable strategies for improvement. These tools can send reminders, collect feedback, and offer personalized recommendations to enhance employee performance.

Hilke Schellmann describes in her book, *The Algorithm*, how Alight combines claims, wealth, HR, and search data to predict the needs of employees. Imagine having personalized recommendations based on who you have added or taken off your insurance plan. Recommendations for doctors are based on care quality and cost. The company said it'd be investing even more heavily to predict mental health issues and musculoskeletal problems before claims are filed.

If this seems creepy, some organizations go a step further than Alight: tracking brains for safety. SmartCap is a tool that tracks truck drivers' alertness and sends an audio-visual signal to the driver when it detects fatigue.[7] Additionally, vocal biomarker tools leverage AI to find signals of mental health problems in voices. The underlying biological components rather than words are analyzed. Companies in this space are trying to find an equivalent of heart rate or blood pressure monitoring for psychiatry.

The use of AI-powered tools to enhance workplace belonging and inclusion is an exciting development. As we move forward, it's essential to prioritize ethical considerations, ensure accountability, and promote transparency. A balanced approach is a must.

Responsible AI and the Role of Trust

When CEOs mandated the return to office, there was constant debate around how to make sure employees are engaged and productive. Many solutions track employees' activity remotely on not only laptops but also company provided or managed cell phones. Zoom initially offered an attendee attention tracking feature, where if Zoom was not the application in focus on a participant's computer for more than 30 seconds while someone else was sharing their screen, Zoom showed a clock icon next to the participant's name in the participant panel.[8]

If you've never heard of this, it's because the feature was short-lived. This feature received significant backlash after the launch. The Zoom team later apologized for falling short of the community's privacy and security expectations and decided to remove the attention tracker feature permanently.

During the pandemic, I remember being asked to measure productivity. The debates would almost never end. Is it as simple as revenue per employee on average within a business unit? What about the support function employees like IT and HR? How would you measure the legal team's productivity? We'd go down a rabbit hole and end up agreeing to focus only on the revenue generating employees in commercial functions because of the ease of obtaining sales-related metrics. For tech companies, engineering teams would use metrics related to code written as a productivity measure. For managers, there might be proxies for manager effectiveness through surveys, but those were not done on a regular basis, so it made for a poor metric. None of these flexible and creative measurements really solved the problem that we couldn't find a single metric that worked for every employee in the company at all times. At times leaders would start thinking about the other side of the productivity spectrum: what if we instead measure how often employees are unproductive?

Because more people are working from home now, companies that didn't traditionally feel the need to track workers started to invest in employee monitoring tools. In April 2020, global demand for employee monitoring software more than doubled.[9] Online searches for "how to monitor employees working from home" increased by 1,705%, and sales for systems that track workers' activity via desktop monitoring, keystroke tracking, video surveillance, GPS location tracking, and other digital tools skyrocketed.

What effect do you think monitoring has on employees' productivity? A 2022 *Harvard Business Review* article states that employee monitoring can improve productivity when used correctly.[10] However, monitoring can also have negative effects on employees, such as reducing their sense of responsibility and agency, which could lead to more rule breaking. In the study, employees who were told they were being monitored were actually more likely to cheat than those who didn't think they were being monitored. Those who were monitored were more likely to report that the authority figure overseeing their surveillance was responsible for their behavior, while the employees who weren't monitored were more likely to take responsibility for their actions. To mitigate these risks, *Harvard Business Review* recommends that leaders treat employees fairly, promote accountability, and present monitoring as a tool to empower employees, not punish them.

If you are new to AI, you might be wondering whether AI is really that different from other technology or traditional software. In certain aspects, the short answer is yes. AI presents a new wave of risks that go beyond traditional software, impacting not just individual companies but entire industries and society as a whole. While AI offers immense potential, it also introduces complexities and uncertainties that current risk frameworks struggle to address.

The biggest challenge lies in the data itself. AI systems are highly reliant on data, but these data can be biased, inaccurate, or outdated, leading to unreliable and potentially harmful output and outcomes. Furthermore, the sheer scale and complexity of AI systems, with millions or even billions of decision points, make it difficult to predict and manage potential problems. Existing frameworks for managing cybersecurity and privacy risks can be adapted to address AI, but they are not sufficient to handle the unique challenges of bias, generative AI, and emerging security threats. Organizations implementing AI need to develop new, comprehensive frameworks that specifically address these risks.

Overall, we must maintain a balanced approach to using AI in the workplace. The next few chapters in this book will provide more detailed discussions on the topic.

Who Is This Book For?

- Business leaders and executives who want to create a more inclusive and healthy workplace culture
- HR professionals who are responsible for well-being, diversity, equity, and inclusion initiatives and want to leverage data analytics to improve their programs
- Data scientists and analytics professionals who want to use data and analytics to drive business decisions and improve workplace culture
- AI and machine learning professionals who are interested in using AI-powered tools to support employee well-being and inclusion

Why This Book Now?

As I reflect on my journey, I've come to realize the profound impact of data-driven approaches on creating inclusive and well-being focused workplaces. Having spent more than a decade navigating the complexities of large global organizations, I've seen firsthand the power of data and AI in driving meaningful change. From my early days at GE to leadership roles at Kraft Heinz and PayPal, I've had the privilege of developing and implementing strategies to measure and improve DEI and ESG initiatives.

Beyond my corporate experience, I've had the opportunity to share my knowledge through teaching and speaking engagements. I've taught courses on people analytics for LinkedIn Learning, focusing on the intersection of DEI, employee well-being, and data-driven talent decisions. Additionally, I've personally contributed to the National Alliance on Mental Illness's efforts to promote workplace mental health.

Throughout my career, I've noticed a recurring theme: many DEI and well-being practitioners possess a wealth of experience but may lack the technical skills to leverage data analytics effectively. On the other hand, analytics professionals often have strong technical expertise but may not fully understand the nuances of DEI and well-being. This book aims to bridge this gap, providing a comprehensive guide for organizations seeking to use data and AI to create more inclusive and supportive workplaces.

While there are numerous books on DEI and well-being, few delve into the critical intersection between these two areas. My research and personal experience have shown me that organizations that prioritize DEI often see improvements in employee well-being. This is not a coincidence. When employees feel seen, heard, and valued, they are more likely to be engaged, productive, and motivated.

The rest of the book is organized as follows:

Chapters 1 through 4 will discuss in detail the "how" of measuring what might seem difficult to measure, DEI and well-being; how to tell stories with these data; and the interconnectedness of DEI and well-being. We will also discuss how to demonstrate the ROI of programs to secure additional funding in a corporate setting. Case studies from prominent organizations will provide additional guidance on the most practical path forward.

We can't talk about data without discussing how AI will impact DEI and well-being. It is a double-edged sword. On the one hand, AI enables quicker analytics and new ways of measuring inclusion and well-being. On the other hand, we have seen headlines around biases in AI that impact hiring, and the AI-created or AI-altered images on social media causing damage for a teen's body image. Chapters 5 and 6 will provide a balanced view of AI's long-term impact and address how to stay human-centered in the age of AI.

What Will You Be Able to Do After Reading?

You are about to dive into a book that will elevate your organization's profitability and productivity. After reading this book, you will have the tools to build a workforce that is not only diverse but also innovative and energized.

First, you will learn how to accurately measure the seemingly "unmeasurable" in the workplace, from inclusion to mental well-being. You will gain skills to quantify the key factors driving inclusion and employee well-being in your organization. With these insights, you will be able to take a data-informed approach to creating a thriving workforce. However, this book is not about crunching numbers. You will also learn how to leverage advanced analytics and AI to uncover opportunities to improve DEI and well-being metrics in meaningful ways that move the needle.

Where it gets more powerful is mapping out integrated strategies that account for the link between an inclusive culture and a healthy employee base. You will use data and AI to finally put a stop to siloed DEI and well-being efforts because there is no well-being without inclusion.

Furthermore, you will gain expertise in quantifying the ROI of your DEI and well-being initiatives. By employing analytical techniques, you will be able to translate the benefits of a diverse and healthy workplace into concrete metrics that resonate with C-level leaders for sustained investment in these critical areas.

Finally, you will see how AI, when used properly, can help you stay ahead of your competitors. In a rapidly changing landscape, building a truly inclusive and well-being-focused workplace and prioritizing human skills that are AI-proof, will be drivers for success. This book is your practical roadmap to positioning your organization for long-term profitability.

Are you ready?

Let's dive in!

Notes

1. The New Era of Leadership. (2024). *Chief.* Available at: https://thenew era.chief.com/research/

2. Berkel, H. (2023). *The healing effects of social connection and community—The coalition to end social isolation and loneliness.* Available at: https://www.endsocialisolation.org/the-healing-effects-of-social-connection-and-community/

3. Valtorta, N.K., Kanaan, M., Gilbody, S., Ronzi, S., and Hanratty, B. (2016). Loneliness and social isolation as risk factors for coronary heart disease and stroke: Systematic review and meta-analysis of longitudinal observational studies. *Heart* 102(13), pp. 1009–1016. doi:https://doi.org/10.1136/heartjnl-2015-308790

4. CARE Rapid Gender Analysis. (2020). *Filling the data gap to build back equal.* Available at: https://www.care.org/wp-content/uploads/2020/09/RGA_SheToldUsSo_9.18.20.pdf

5. Vance, T.A. (2019). *Addressing mental health in the Black Community.* Columbia University Department of Psychiatry. Available at: https://www.columbiapsychiatry.org/news/addressing-mental-health-black-community

6. Smith, G. and Rustagi, I. (2022). Workplace AI wants to help you belong. *Stanford Social Innovation Review.* Available at: https://ssir.org/articles/entry/workplace_ai_wants_to_help_you_belong

7. Weed, J. (2020). Wearable tech that tells drowsy truckers it's time to pull over. *New York Times.* 6 Feb. Available at: https://www.nytimes.com/2020/02/06/business/drowsy-driving-truckers.html?

8. Li, T.W., Arya, A., and Jin, H. (2024). Redesigning privacy with user feedback: The case of zoom attendee attention tracking. *Proceedings of the 2024 CHI Conference on Human Factors in Computing Systems* (237), 1–14. https://doi.org/10.1145/3613904.3642594

9. Ball, K. (2021). *Electronic monitoring and surveillance in the workplace.* JRC Publications Repository. Available at: https://publications.jrc.ec.europa.eu/repository/handle/JRC125716

10. Thiel, C., Bonner, J.M., Bush, J., Welsh, D., and Garud, N. (2022). Monitoring employees makes them more likely to break rules. *Harvard Business Review.* Available at: https://hbr.org/2022/06/monitoring-employees-makes-them-more-likely-to-break-rules

Chapter 1
The Power of Data and AI in DEI and Well-being

Have you heard of the glass ceiling? How about the bamboo ceiling? These are references to barriers for women and Asians to be promoted into senior leadership roles in organizations, respectively. Have you ever wondered if such a "ceiling" existed in your organization? How would you measure that? Let's start by going through the measurement of diversity in an organization.

Diversity Measurement

Measuring diversity doesn't have to be complicated. As the former head of People Analytics, I've created the measurement strategy for diversity and DEI (diversity, equity, and inclusion) reporting at Fortune 500 companies. At times, I started from scratch with no previous measures, and at others I revamped the outdated measurements. Getting started doesn't have to be daunting.

Representation

How do you get started in measuring diversity? Representation is a great place to start, since it provides a snapshot of the organization's current state. This enables you to quickly answer questions such as, "How many female leaders do we have?" and "What percentage of our engineering organization is Black?"

1

If you are starting to measure representation, there are two considerations to keep in mind: dimension and segment.

The first consideration is around the **dimension** of diversity your organization wants to measure. Gender, race, ethnicity, age, LGBTQ+ status, veteran status, and disability status are some of the most common ones. Your leadership team and the board of directors may also focus on different dimensions.

The second question considers for which **segment** these metrics are important. Common segments may include levels, functions, business units, and locations.

Job levels can include categories such as vice president, director, manager, and so on. Functions may be as simple as tech versus non-tech or can include granular descriptions such as sales, marketing, engineering, finance, IT, and HR. Locations can take on regions, countries, and cities.

The combination of dimensions and segments will allow you to answer detailed questions such as, "What percentage of managers, senior managers, directors, vice presidents, and executive leadership team are women?" to help inform whether there is a glass ceiling in your organization.

A common question I answered while working in the tech industry is, "What percentage of tech and non-tech positions consist of women?" This may not be as relevant if your organization isn't in the tech industry, but there can be other job function segments that are relevant. If you look at the diversity reports from large global tech companies, such as Google, these are common dimensions and segmentations.[1]

While gender is a dimension that is globally consistent, race and ethnicity may require a more regional or country specific approach. There may be locations where race and ethnicity are more homogeneous or where ethnicity takes on a different meaning. This is why many organizations I have worked with choose to limit the race and ethnicity measurement to their US locations.

As I review the diversity data for various other global organizations, the decision may have to do with the context of race and ethnicity rather than not having diverse employee population to warrant such measurement globally. Some of the largest global organizations, Microsoft and Walmart, for example, disclose race and ethnicity for US-based employees. Google, on the other hand, publishes race and ethnicity data for each region, including Americas, Asia-Pacific, and EMEA (Europe, Middle East, and Africa).

In summary, to get started with diversity representation you need the minimum of gender, race, ethnicity, age or generation, and veteran status to paint a picture of the workforce. The additional data on LGBTQ+ status and disability status are also helpful if available in the organization.

How often should you refresh the diversity data? I recommend monitoring and updating the metrics of interest quarterly. For large organizations or those going through significant change, monthly would be a more appropriate frequency. Of course, the most ideal scenario is to refresh daily so metrics are available in near real time. However, that may not be realistic for analytics teams that are just getting started nor should they be considered a deal breaker if daily updates aren't available. In global organizations where such data are not stored in the HR system but instead have to be obtained via anonymous surveys due to legal reasons, an annual refresh may be the most realistic option given the time commitment.

Now that you know how to measure representation, what are some ways to improve it?

There are three key levers that can move the needle on diversity representation: **hiring, promotion,** and **retention**.

Hiring Diversity

Let's dive into the first lever, hiring. How do you measure the diversity in hiring? Hiring diversity is the diversity of your organization's new hires over a period. For gender diversity in hiring, for instance, you'll want to know what percentage of the new hires consist of women, men, and non-binary. If nothing else changes, hiring more women will improve the overall female representation number. If that seems too easy, it's because we're not done yet. You may receive questions from hiring managers or the HR leadership team. Why are we hiring so few women in engineering? It is useful to have measurement throughout the entire recruitment funnel.

Before diving into the data, you want to start with a focused and concrete problem to solve. For example, here are some questions I've seen organizations ask frequently.

- Are there any bottlenecks in the recruitment process that require immediate attention?
- Where do applicants who identify as woman drop off in the process?
- Which recruiting source brings in the highest acceptance rates among women?

A recruitment funnel, or hiring funnel, outlines each stage of the recruitment process, from sourcing candidates to onboarding. As you overlay the diversity dimension and source information onto the recruitment funnel, you'll be able to answer the second and third questions we just discussed. Here's why these questions are helpful: Imagine if you found out from the gender recruitment funnel analysis that women tend to drop off between qualified and interview stages. You could further examine if there are biases in an interview selection process. Alternatively, you might discover that women were less likely to make it to the final hired stage. This data might prompt follow-up questions such as, "Are women less likely to accept a job offer, or are they less likely to be offered?"

Identifying bias in a specific stage can be challenging, given the number of factors involved. You can review interview feedback or interview assessment scores by gender if such data are available. However, it is often challenging to get a clear reason why an offer is rejected because many candidates don't want to burn the bridge. There may also be multiple reasons, making it difficult to pinpoint a single factor.

Let's imagine your data shows that female applicants who apply via LinkedIn are the most likely to become a successful hire, whereas referrals are the least effective. Is it time to reconsider the sourcing strategy?

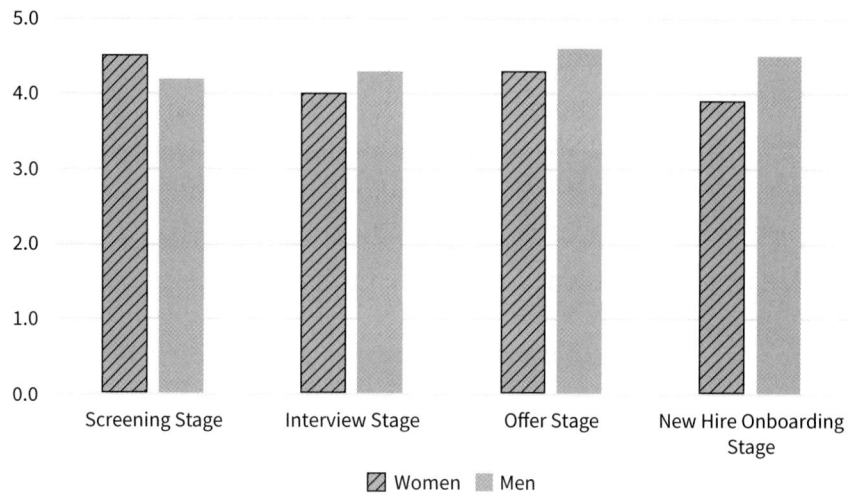

Figure 1.1 Candidate Feedback Data by Gender Across Recruitment Stages

One underrated data source in the recruitment process is the *Candidate Experience Survey data.* Think back to your own experience as a candidate. Would you accept a job offer when you were treated poorly?

This data can shed light on whether applicants from different backgrounds experience the recruiting process differently. When you compare the survey results by dimension of diversity such as gender, you can also look at the results within each stage of the recruitment process.

You can put the candidate feedback data by stage on a single chart and compare across demographic groups, as shown in Figure 1.1, for instance[2]:

What do you observe in this chart? While women report higher satisfaction levels during the screening stage, their satisfaction drops during the subsequent stages of the hiring process. In addition to the qualitative scores, it's also important to analyze the survey comments to fully understand the candidate experience for various groups. We will discuss more about how to analyze comments later in this chapter.

Attrition Diversity

Another lever an organization can use to improve representation is retention, or attrition prevention. Should you care about the diversity of the employees who have left your organization? Sometimes described as the "leaky bucket" issue in DEI, attrition of diverse talent is one of the reasons many organizations haven't made significant progress.

If the number of women your organization has hired is similar to or lower than the number of women leaving the company, there will be no progress in the female representation. This is why it's critical to also measure attrition diversity.

How do you measure attrition diversity? Similar to the promotion diversity, you will measure the attrition rate for each group.

In the 2022 McKinsey and Lean In study, 10.5% of women leaders quit their jobs over the last year, which was the highest rate since 2017.[3] In contrast, the rate for men was only 9%. The report said the attrition rates for men and women run closer together historically, with a spread of only around half a point.

You can perform the same calculation for other diversity dimensions and see if employees of a particular race and ethnicity leave the company at a higher rate. It is important to separate the type of employee exits and focus on what is in the organization's control to improve, voluntary attrition or resignations and not retirements or other involuntary reductions in force.

What can you do if you identify a gap in the attrition rates of different groups? You can compare the leaving reasons in exit surveys or interviews for the various groups to better understand why. Are women or men more likely to leave for compensation reasons? Are millennials more likely to leave for flexibility than other generations? Are Black directors more likely to leave for career growth than White directors?

If you do not have exit survey data, it can still be helpful to talk to employees to understand their decision to leave and experience while working in the organization. Some organizations choose to have HR business partners conduct exit conversations instead of sending out exit surveys. This can be particularly helpful with contextual information surveys cannot capture.

Here are some sample questions:

- What made you start looking for another role?
  - If you didn't proactively look for another role but were instead contacted by a recruiter, what made you take the call?
- Prior to accepting the new job offer, did you look into options that would make it possible for you to stay here?
- Did you feel like your job description or responsibilities have changed since you were hired? If so, in which ways?
- Were you given the tools and resources to be successful here? If not, what could have been improved to make it better?
- Are there any concerns or issues you'd like to share?
- What are you most looking forward to in your new role?

Promotion Diversity

Since career growth is an important part of why employees join and leave companies, it is another lever for increasing diversity representation.

How do you measure diversity in the promotion process? You can get a baseline understanding by looking at the diversity representation by level and see where women or people of color appear to face a ceiling.

To take it a step further, you'll want to look at the rate of promotion for different diversity dimensions. The question you'll want to consider is, "**Are certain groups less likely to be promoted than others?**"

As the 2024 Women in the Workplace report states, "Women continue to face barriers at the beginning of the pipeline. They remain *less* likely than men to be hired into entry-level roles, which leaves them underrepresented from the start. Then, women are far less likely than men to attain their very first promotion to a manager role—a situation that's not improving. In 2018, for every 100 men who received their first promotion to manager in 2018, 79 women were promoted; this year, just 81 women were."[4]

The report further shows this first promotion to manager barrier, called the "broken rung" is even worse for women of color. For every 100 men promoted to manager, 89 White women were promoted in 2024. Asian women have experienced the greatest improvements in the "broken rung" but encounter significant hurdles later in the pipeline at more senior roles. After notable improvements in 2021 and 2022, Black women's promotion rates this year regressed to 2020 levels. In 2024, Latinas faced their worst broken rung. For every 100 men promoted to manager, only 65 Latinas were promoted in 2024.

For the promotion diversity analysis in your organization, it is helpful to segment it by level as well and see if the disparity in promotion rates stays consistent or worsens at more senior levels as found in the 2024 Women in the Workplace Report.

When we observe a particular group is less likely to be promoted, the natural question is why? One way to understand this is to look at the processes **before** promotion decisions are made.

For instance, is there a gap in the performance evaluation between men and women? Are the high potential programs balanced in terms of demographic backgrounds? A study by an MIT Sloan professor found the gender gap in promotion can be explained by women receiving substantially lower potential ratings.[5] What's more, relative to men with the same scores for potential, women outperformed their previous year's score, yet they were still given lower potential ratings heading into the next year.

Another analysis you can do for promotion is to compare how long employees have been working at their current level across demographic groups. Have women been at the manager level longer than men on average? When you are working with this data, be careful not to use time-in-job but use time-in-grade or time-in-level instead, since lateral moves could be miscalculated.

While you could look at how long employees were at their prior level for those who got promoted, note this comparison ignores those who weren't promoted completely, which arguably is a larger issue.

Legal Concerns

Depending on the roles and responsibilities, some organizations have established compensation teams that will run this type of analysis in-house or partner with external firms to do so. Other organizations have their people analytics team run the analysis with the in-house labor and employment legal team overseeing the effort. One thing I highly recommend as a former labor and employment litigation consultant is to never run your own promotion and pay equity analysis without having the in-house legal team's blessing. You could be creating discoverable evidence unintentionally.

A more advanced application of people analytics in this space is to leverage text analytics on the performance evaluations to see whether there are differences in the sentiment and themes by group. If the performance ratings are similar between women and men, for instance, but the text reveals something drastically different, it could be useful to include in understanding the promotion disparity. Again, given the sensitivity of performance data, it is important to check with your legal counsel before running any analysis.

Are organizations required to report on diversity numbers? To some extent, yes. The US federal law requires employers with 100 or more employees to submit workforce data to the Equal Employment Opportunity Commission (EEOC). The data collected includes workforce information by job category and sex, race, or ethnicity. Many organizations that share diversity stats publicly go beyond the EEOC requirements in those public reports. Additionally, the Securities and Exchange Commission (SEC) introduced new disclosure requirements in 2020 designed to provide stakeholders insight into human capital. The disclosures may help stakeholders evaluate whether a business has the right workforce to meet immediate and emerging business challenges and the nature and magnitude of the related investments. In certain SEC filings, a public company is now required to disclose (1) the number of employees and a description of its human capital resources, if material to the business as a whole, and if material to a particular segment, that segment should be identified; and (2) any human capital measures or objectives, if material, that the registrant focuses on in managing its business, such as those related to the development, attraction, safety, engagement, and retention of employees.

Whether required by law or not, investors are increasingly demanding transparency from companies on their talent processes and data.

Inclusion and Well-being Measurement

Diversity may be the more visible and quantifiable concept, but what about inclusion and well-being? It is certainly less straightforward to measure inclusion than diversity and well-being.

Think about the last time you felt excluded at work.

What happened? Was there a meeting you felt like you should have been part of? Did someone make a decision that impacted you without your input? Was there an after-work casual gathering that you wish you were invited to? Was it yet another conversation about a high school reunion because most of your colleagues graduated from the same high school? Was there a conversation about vacations, and you felt utterly out of place because your colleagues described activities so out of your budget?

Now, think about how you would quantify the level of inclusion you experienced.

There are two ways of gathering quantitative data on inclusion and well-being: actively and passively.

Active Data Gathering: Survey Design and Implementation

Inclusion and well-being can be measured through an index of multiple questions on a survey or as simply as one single question.

There is not a single question that is best for all companies, therefore I'd recommend getting alignment with senior stakeholders beforehand. Specifically, there are three questions to align on:

1. Why are we measuring inclusion and well-being as an organization? Whether it's a request from the board of directors or

because employees have reported feeling excluded, the reason can shape your measurement approach differently. Think about this question as a way to help you write a problem statement for the survey design.

2. What questions measure the inclusion and well-being at work? This is the "how" in measurement. Sometimes organizations can overthink this, so I encourage the survey design team to anchor to the "why" in the previous question. The measures do not need to capture every dimension of inclusion and well-being. It is critical to focus on addressing the "why" instead. In a global organization, for instance, it's important to run the translated questions by a few local representatives to ensure it means what it's intended to mean.

3. What will we do with this data? Most importantly, you want to ensure the organization is ready to take action on the data once collected. If the answer is "nothing" or "we are just curious," consider having a serious discussion on the accountability of action planning/taking. My number one rule for survey design is that every question will be actionable—and if the organization will not change regardless of the feedback from employees, that question should be removed from the survey.

Bonus! The quantitative answers often don't provide the context of the response. You can add an optional text box to capture open responses after each survey question so a respondent can provide additional information if they choose to.

Before we dive into how to design surveys, let's talk about a phrase that has been surfaced in the news in recent years: "toxic culture." We have seen employees describe toxic bosses and toxic culture in detail on TikTok and YouTube. Some cite this toxicity as the reason for mental health struggles, burnout, and eventually leaving their job. It makes us wonder: Can toxic culture be measured?

The short answer is yes.

According to the research by Donald Sull and his coauthors on "Why Every Leader Needs to Worry About Toxic Culture," a toxic culture consists of five elements: lack of inclusion, disrespect, cutthroat behavior, abusive management, and unethical behavior.

Data are particularly helpful because they can pinpoint where the toxicity is in the organization. Sull's research shows that toxicity is often concentrated in specific teams, divisions, or regions, within otherwise healthy cultures. It can also enable analysis of toxicity experience by demographic groups, including gender, race/ethnicity, and more. In the data from global companies I've seen, it's common for different groups to have different experiences.

Research shows that between 2006 and 2021, women were 35% more likely to mention toxic culture in their negative Glassdoor reviews compared with men.[6] The pandemic may have widened the toxic culture gender gap, as women were 41% more likely to suffer toxicity in the workplace in the first year after the onset of COVID-19. This toxic culture gender gap does not appear to diminish with seniority. Across self-reported C-level roles, women were 53% more likely to experience toxicity than men.

Another concept that comes up a lot in discussions around DEI is psychological safety. Several years ago, the Google Aristotle project found that psychological safety was the primary factor that differentiates high-performing teams from low-performing ones. Since then, there has been an increased focus on how to create psychologically safe work environments. To be able to encourage diverse and innovative perspectives, employees must feel safe enough to challenge the status quo, take risks, and potentially fail. Amy Edmondson, author of *The Fearless Organization*, lists out seven statements to measure this concept:

1. If you make a mistake on this team, it is often held against you.
2. Members of this team are able to bring up problems and tough issues.
3. People on this team sometimes reject others for being different.
4. It is safe to take a risk on this team.
5. It is difficult to ask other members of this team for help.
6. No one on this team would deliberately act in a way that undermines my efforts.
7. Working with members of this team, my unique skills and talents are valued and utilized.

One of my favorite reminders from Amy's book is that "psychological safety is not about being nice." Having psychological safety isn't a guarantee that all your ideas will be applauded and there won't be disagreements or conflicts. According to Amy, psychological safety is "a belief that neither the formal nor informal consequences of interpersonal risks, like asking for help or admitting a failure, will be punitive."

When Amy studied medical errors at a university hospital, she found that detected error rates depended on only on the actual error rates but also the rate of reporting. Teams with poor communication were making more errors but were too afraid to report them, due to the lack of psychological safety.[7]

Let's reflect for a moment. When was the last time your team made a mistake? What did you do as a team leader? It is actually unnatural to not care about others' perception of you at work. After all, our career and our future depend on it. One of the questions I always ask when I join a new organization or start leading a new team is, "When was the last time our team took a risk?" The risk itself tells you what is considered risky in this environment, and what happens after the risk was taken tells you the level of psychological safety. Another important aspect of psychological safety is that it can make or break the performance of a diverse team. Research has shown that expertise-diverse teams perform well when psychological safety is high and badly otherwise.[8]

Given the role of psychological safety in team performance and innovation, as illustrated in the previous research, it is critical to measure and monitor psychological safety in your organization.

Once you have a clear measure of psychological safety, it can be helpful to consider adding the measure to employee engagement surveys or 360 and leadership effectiveness surveys. When these data are captured on a regular basis; you can further analyze the relationship between psychological safety and other measures, such as well-being.

Now that you have an idea of the analysis you'll do, let's think about the survey design.

Survey Design

When you hear the word survey, do you immediately think of a long employee survey with 50+ questions or something short and sweet? This likely depends on your own experience and the companies you have worked with. A survey can be a single question or 100+ questions long.

Why does the length of a survey matter? There is often a trade-off between length of survey and participation since no one wants to spend time answering 100 questions. However, in my experience, I've found the willingness to participate is more about the content of the questions than the length.

Put yourself in the employees' shoes for a moment. What would make you want to provide feedback on a survey? The questions are relevant to your life, and you believe someone will take action on your feedback. Instead of being worried about how many questions would be appropriate, focus on the themes of the survey to ensure the survey objectives will be achieved. For instance, if you set out to measure A, B, and C, make sure those topics are covered.

What about the frequency of surveys? The frequency of surveys does not matter as much as you think. Think about the last time you took an Uber—did it send you a quick survey to rate the experience? I bet you took it even though it's the same question and very frequent if you use Uber a lot. Why do you continue to provide feedback? Of course, yes, it's a quick 5-star rating, but more importantly, you fundamentally believe it somewhat matters for your future experience! The Uber survey is a two-way street so there are plenty of incentives for you to answer and hopefully, a 5-star rating will match you with great drivers in the future.

How do you determine the right frequency of employee surveys in an organization? One of the key factors is how quickly actions can be taken based on the survey feedback. You want to give employees the chance to see if their feedback was considered before asking them the same questions in another survey.

Here is a sample survey with DEI and well-being focus:

Engagement/Intent to Stay

- I see myself working here 1 year from now.
- I would recommend this as a great place to work.

Career—Equity

- I have opportunities to advance here.
- My manager offers equal opportunities to people of different backgrounds.

Manager

- My manager cares about me as a person.

Inclusion

- I am included in important discussions that impact me at work.

Well-being

- I have energy to do things I enjoy after I am finished with my workday.
- My company offers benefits to help with my well-being.

As mentioned before, give respondents the opportunity to comment after each question so you can get additional context. This short survey provides an example of how you can collect data on a wide range of topics in a relatively short amount of time.

We will discuss program evaluations later in the book. For now, keep in mind that these types of surveys can be conducted before and after an inclusion or well-being program implementation to gauge the impact.

"The Price of Not Knowing"

I was leading people analytics at one of the largest global food companies in the world when COVID-19 hit. The world had shut down in an instant, and our food items were flying off the grocery store shelves. As the majority of the company's employees had to keep working to produce food for the world, health and safety quickly became the number one concern for the CEO and board of directors. We also started to hear how isolating it was to be stuck in a tiny apartment in large cities, especially the employees who live alone. To better understand the health and well-being of employees, my team designed and launched the first-ever Health and Well-being Survey in the company's history.

The leadership team debated whether to open up the office for employees who need space to go into the office. This was before the return-to-office debate started. Ultimately the feedback from employees who need an alternative space to work got the leaders to choose partially opening the headquarters office with protocols in place, including attestation health forms, sanitation measures, and social distancing.

One of the hurdles in the implementation was pushback from the legal and privacy teams. "What if they disclosed personal problems we cannot help with?" "What if someone accidentally shares their private health information, such as health conditions?"

We demonstrated the price of not knowing was too high during such a critical time.

Survey Implementation

Once you have designed the survey and aligned with stakeholders on launching it, the implementation work begins. There are several decisions you will need to make in this process. Following are the key aspects to consider in the implementation.

Confidential or Anonymous?

Should you keep the survey completely anonymous or confidential? What is the difference? An anonymous survey means you won't be able to identify individual respondents at all, while confidential means the individual results are protected but the survey vendor or administrator has access to individual responses under certain circumstances. I generally recommend confidential rather than anonymous surveys because of the rare occasions when you need to identify an employee who is either at risk to themselves or to another colleague. While surveys are not meant for such purposes, occasionally employees without other outlets might treat the survey as the outlet to share. Comments that reference severe mental health and unethical behaviors would require immediate intervention. There is no right or wrong way to design a survey, and this requires a strategic discussion at the senior leadership level, informed by the company's legal, compliance, and risk tolerance.

What guardrails should you consider?

If employees feel like their answers would be traced back to them, it will be difficult to receive responses that aren't sugar-coated. Be aware of how the survey is perceived in the organization. One thing I wish I had spent more time on early in my People Analytics leader journey is understanding how employees and managers think of the past surveys. If the perception might be "waste of time" or "check the box," you'll have your work cut out for you before launching another survey. On the other hand, if it's an effort managers and employees across the organization truly support, it's easier to continue these feedback gathering activities.

Optics

Should the survey announcement come from the CEO or the CHRO? It sends a different tone when the CEO is the one who announces the importance of listening to employees. Employee surveys often risk the reputation of "an HR thing to do" rather than the truly strategic data gathering it is. My recommendation to organizations is to follow what is authentic to your leadership team. If it is something the CEO genuinely cares about, then the communication should come from the CEO. Employees see right through inauthentic statements especially when it is not backed by actions.

Tactical Reminders

Should you launch the survey to every employee at the same time centrally or at the same time locally? Depending on how many offices you have across the world, it may be helpful to have the survey launch in the morning for everyone participating, or at least not have anyone receive the invite to participate in the middle of the night their time to maximize participation rates.

Don't forget to do the safelisting and testing beforehand. The survey vendor may be able to help with testing but your central survey team should always test it to ensure the survey functions as expected and any company communications are sent at the right time.

Action Planning and Taking

Some might call this the *real work* in any survey process. Of course, the design, launch, and analysis take a lot of effort, but a survey is not successful if no actions are taken on the results. Action planning and taking is the critical step where many organizations struggle.

There are two typical approaches to action planning: Top-down or bottom-up.

Top-down action planning means the CEO lays out a high-level plan aiming to improve certain areas based on the survey findings, then each C-level leader creates a more detailed plan to execute on the CEO's plan.

On the other hand, the bottom-up approach means each business unit or even manager creates a plan based on their survey results and shares those upward with their leaders.

In either scenario, it takes a long time for the entire organization to create a holistic action plan and execute it. The bottom-up approach is sometimes faster if managers start working on their plans locally without having to wait for senior leadership approval. The top-down approach, on the other hand, is often great for accountability.

Which one should you choose? It will depend on your culture. Certain organizations do better with a top-down approach while others with a bottom-up approach. The CEO's willingness to engage also matters. You won't successfully have a top-down approach if the CEO is not willing to be involved.

There is a risk with the bottom-up approach that is worth noting. Often an organization's survey will have at least 20 questions on various items and themes and the action planning will focus on the three lowest or most impactful items. As you can imagine, these three items may be different at different levels of the organization. There is a chance that every business unit ends up working on three different items if they work in silos. For instance, if the Engineering division works on Career Development, Work Life Balance, and Inclusion while the Finance division works on Manager Effectiveness, Collaboration, and Communication, the overall organization may see a slight improvement in all six areas but not enough to move the needle overall.

What holds organizations back? Several factors hold organizations back from taking action on their surveys:

1. Inability to agree due to analysis paralysis.
2. The plan is too complicated to execute.
3. The leadership team made other big changes such as layoffs that "offset" the plan.
4. Lack of analytical capabilities to compile insights from survey data.

How can you avoid these pitfalls?

- Align with the leadership team before survey launch with key dates.
- Ensure the analytics team knows what they'll take on beforehand and have capacity.

While there will likely never be a time when your organization isn't "too busy for an employee survey," there can be times when you can expect more clashing of priorities than others. You don't need the survey to be the sole focus during that week or month, but you can avoid making it the lowest priority to ensure participation and meaningful discussions. If a giant merger has just been announced, it may be helpful to wait until the dust settles a little before launching a survey.

Confidential Surveys

Mary leads the employee survey team at a large consumer goods company. It's the busiest time of the year for her team, since the engagement survey just closed. Her team was heads down, analyzing the freshly gathered data, and noticed a comment that stopped them in their tracks.

"There is no point to any of this. I sometimes think about how much easier it would be if I ended my life."

Because the survey was confidential, it was difficult to track down who wrote it. Mary immediately alerts the HR team and then contacts the survey vendor to see how they could uncover the identity of the employee who needs help. At this point, the company's legal and privacy team is engaged to ensure the company can reach the employee as quickly as possible legally while protecting the employee's privacy.

This is an example of where a survey decision is not as straightforward.

Vendor Selection for Employee Surveys

After running a few requests for proposals (RFPs) for survey vendors, I've learned from experience what makes a successful implementation.

First, be clear on which criteria you will use to evaluate the vendors:

- Type of surveys needed (Employee experience, candidate experience, post-training questionnaire, 360 leadership assessments, etc.)
- Features (Mobile friendly, QR code deployment)
- Reporting and analytics capabilities
- Integration with the human resource information system, applicant tracking system, learning management system
- Global/culture/languages/translation
- Survey design expertise (Do we have it in house or will we rely on the vendor?)

Ask yourself the following questions as things to consider:

- How do we currently measure employee experience?
- How are we currently capturing candidate experience and learner feedback? (These are important if you want the survey vendor to be able to provide both.)
- How soon do we need to launch the next employee survey? (Implementation time)
- Who provides input and signs off on the survey questions in the company? Is this a complex and lengthy process where you need the vendor's support when a last minute change is requested?

Contract

Your procurement team will likely have expertise on what contract terms are acceptable. The vendor will often push for multiyear contracts, and this is a point to negotiate if you think there is a possibility of switching after a year. Also, know that the team you meet during the sales process will likely not be the one supporting you after the contract is signed. So if there are specific criteria for the customer success team in terms of expertise or response time, make sure you are including those in the contract. I've used the same survey vendor in different organizations and had a drastically different experience because of the customer success team assigned. Their expertise matters.

Switching Survey Platform?

Once in a while, you might find yourself in a situation where you need to switch vendors. What should you do? My biggest advice is: *Don't start with the tech. Start with the data.*

You will want to ask your stakeholders on what's required for board and compliance reporting along with the appetite for change in measurement, before talking tech changes.

If you are required to produce exactly the same engagement index and year-over-year change to government agencies or the company board of directors, it is critical to ensure the new survey vendor can do this. This means you may need the new vendor to import previous year survey results and create trending analysis in their platform. For such import to be successful, the data columns and dimensions must be set up to accommodate data exports from the current vendor. Is it a simple download and then upload? Or is it a much more complex process? How will you ensure privacy and security of data in this process?

In my experience, most survey vendors have their own engagement index and while some customization is possible, it could mean drastically different measures. Additionally, every vendor argues that their engagement index is the best, so for their own benchmarking purposes, some are unwilling to enable customized engagement metrics even if it's what the customers wanted in order to perform trending analysis.

If trending analysis is not possible within the platform, you need to produce it more manually. This could be a daunting task in large organizations.

General Tips for Success in Implementation of Survey Technology

Whether you are starting from scratch, transitioning from survey monkey, or moving from one large vendor to another, the following tips will help ensure your success:

- **Data-centered:** I don't mean the charts the survey technology can produce. I am referring to focusing on the data you will need before the features of the platform. What questions do you need to be able to answer for the survey to be successful?
- **Prioritize collaboration:** Are there different groups that might want to use the platform? Candidate experience? What other groups need to collaborate or support you for the implementation to be a success? The typical functions you'll need to work closely with are IT, Compliance, and Legal/Privacy.
- **Stakeholder management:** Who makes the decisions ultimately? Who controls the budget for the initial implementation? The scope should be clear. I've seen RFPs go from a simple engagement survey to something that solves world hunger. A survey platform is powerful, but it doesn't need to solve every group's needs right away.
- **Stay curious:** Keep learning and stay connected to practitioners in your industry so you can learn from each other. I don't need to remind you how quickly the world of technology is changing. By staying curious and adopting a growth mindset, you are likely to stay on top of new trends and be able to provide more value to your organization. What's the latest way of measuring employee experience in the hybrid world?
- **Be flexible:** Since change is the only constant, staying flexible can be very helpful during a long implementation process. You might run into unexpected issues such as data quality not being where it needs to be or the customer success team you loved just resigned.

Passive Data

Surveys are not the only way to gather data. You could get a sense of the level of inclusion and well-being through communication patterns. Many employees feel excluded when they are not asked to be in a meeting or decision-making process they wanted to be part of. Communication and collaboration data such as who your manager most frequently interacts with on the team can shed light on how inclusive they are. The passive data gathering process goes around the survey process and directly captures which participants were in the same meeting, how often, for how long, and potentially the topic of the discussion. Yes, I'm referring to meeting, chat, and email metadata.

Inclusion

Organizational network analysis (ONA) can be a useful way to visualize the extent of inclusion in a team. Using the metadata from emails, chats, and calendar invites, ONA shows you which groups and to what extent they have interacted with each other.

You can overlay job-related and demographic data on the graph to answer important questions such as the following:

- Are women or minorities more likely to be excluded from meetings with senior leaders?
- Are new hires or younger generations more likely to be excluded from conversations that impact their career?
- Is there sufficient collaboration across functions and domains when the company is working toward a big shift in strategy that requires it?
- Is there enough discussion between engineering and product organizations related to a new product launch?
- Do sales and marketing teams currently work together?

You can take it a step further and see whether certain groups are excluded from conversations on slack—this can be a great way to see if there's an echo chamber. However, be careful not to jump to conclusions if certain individuals don't participate, because it could reflect their preference of communication channels. Figure 1.2 illustrates gender distribution in a networks with levels as an overlay. This is a graphical analysis that can answer whether there is a difference between women's and men's networks, in terms of

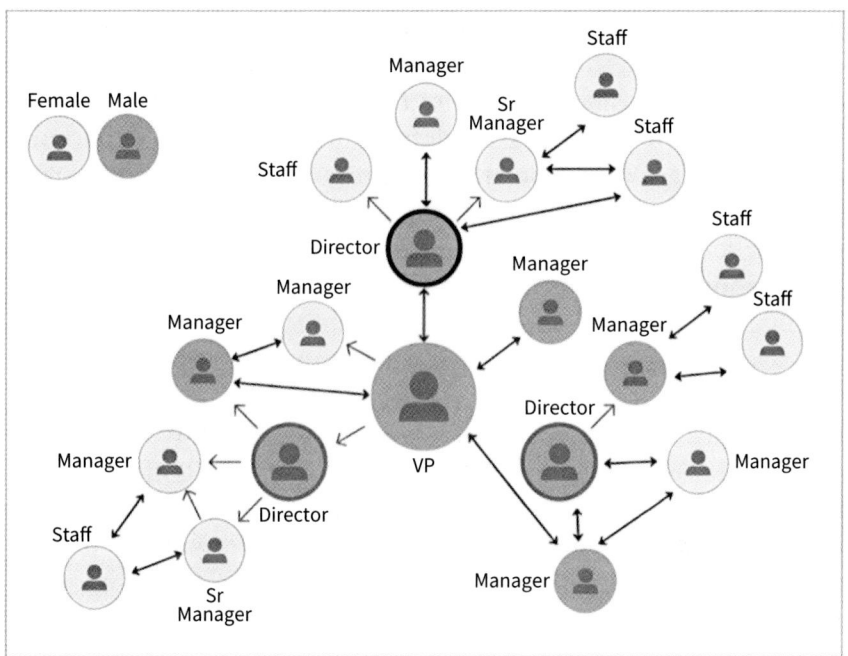

Figure 1.2 Organizational Network Analysis of Gender and Levels

connection and information seeking from senior leaders in the organization. The arrow indicates whether the information seeking behaviors are one-directional or bi-directional. The shade of the icons indicates the gender of the individual. In this hypothetical example, the graph illustrates that not only do men tend to hold the most senior positions but the most senior person, the vice president, is communicating with only one woman. Based on the direction of the arrow, you can see this vice president only asks for information from that one woman, who is a manager, and the woman does not seek or receive information from the vice president.

This figure demonstrates that even without names or content of the communication, ONA can map out where exclusions occur in the organization.

Although many associate ONA with passively collected communication and collaboration data, it is also possible to use ONA with actively collected data. For example, you can ask employees to share names of up to top 25 colleagues who are important in their ability to accomplish work priorities.[9] While passively collected communication data may seem more complete, my experience implementing ONA in large global organizations has been that actively collected data is easier to get past internal legal and privacy reviews, due to the opt-in nature of the collection process.

In addition to virtual meetings and communication patterns, there are in-person events where you can capture inclusive behaviors as well. If your organization hosts company events or other networking functions, it is helpful to understand who signs up and who attends. Take events sponsored by the Employee Resource Group (ERG), for example. If women of color are significantly less likely to show up to events than White women at a Women's Network event designed for everyone at work, for instance, it could be useful to better understand the barriers for them to attend. Are the events truly inclusive? The post-event surveys can also provide additional insights to the participants' experience.

Well-being

When it comes to well-being, there are also burnout signals you can observe in the collaboration data. For instance, how frequently do employees chat or meet outside of normal working hours? How many hours do they spend working, and how long are their days?

The same data where you analyze the touchpoints between leaders and their teams can tell you a lot about both inclusion and well-being. Previous surveys show that managers have more impact on their team's mental health than doctors and therapists. It is not surprising given how much influence our manager has on our professional life. On the one hand, an extreme a micromanager may be contacting their employees multiple times throughout the day, and on the other, an absent manager may go without contacting their team for weeks. Neither situation is likely great for the team's well-being. Of course, every individual has their own preferred style of working, so the management style that works for one employee may not work for another. By overlaying the collaboration and meeting data with survey responses, you can have a more holistic picture of your employees' well-being.

There are also other data sources such as employee assistance programs (EAP) utilization and medical leave that can offer clues to the health and well-being of employees. These sensitive data are often unavailable at the individual level or at least are masked so only aggregated data are available. It can be helpful to analyze the trends of these aggregated data, however. If the percentage of employees taking medical leave has suddenly increased significantly, it is time to dig deeper and understand why.

Wearable Devices at Work

Imagine a world where your employer has access to your heart rate and sleep patterns. Your manager adjusts your workload based on your stress levels. No, it's not in the future. This is from a case study of employees at PwC UK.

In 2019, a pilot group of PwC employees in the UK began wearing devices connected to their work calendars. During the COVID-19 lockdown, PwC UK asked for volunteers to wear a wearable device for comparison with the 2019 baseline. Some of the comparisons between this newly remote workforce and their pre-COVID peer group were unsurprising, such as the 27% drop in daily steps. Other data analytics showed how much back-to-back video calls impacted employees' sleep.

What actions did the firm take with these data? The data painted a clear picture of the conditions that make employees thrive, so PwC adjusted wellness benefits and workload. It also empowered employees to take more breaks throughout the day.

The combination of wearables and work surveillance technology can provide employers with large amounts of data on their employees. The question is no longer if they can but whether they should.

Well-being and Employee Attrition

What do you think is the connection between well-being and employee attrition? If employees are working excessively long hours and on the verge of burnout, they may be more likely to look for new jobs with more work-life balance. For knowledge workers, since they do not typically clock in and out, the passive data on meeting data are a good proxy for hours worked. If employees spend hours of their evening attending meetings or start earlier and end later than normal, it may lead to burnout in the long run. We know that remote work increases the time we spend in meetings, but at what point is it "too much"?[10] In my own analysis of F100 company data, the team level attrition spikes after the work hours lengthen for a prolonged period, though the "tipping point" varies from one organization to another. I'd recommend using at least 6–12 months of data to identify the baseline meeting time and behavior first if you were to conduct this analysis. After all, a team that works with colleagues on the other side of the world may have different hours than those that work with only local colleagues.

Considerations for Using Passive Data

The toughest part about implementing ONA is the legal review you must go through, especially if your employee base is global. Even if no names are ever disclosed in the network data analysis, there are privacy regulations around the globe that can prevent you from using such data.

One of my simple rules is that if you are not going to like the use case to be on the front page of the *New York Times* or *Wall Street Journal*, then it probably needs some more discussion. There is undoubtedly some creepiness with network analysis, even if you know your employer already collects this data on you. The old way of "let's see what the data tells us and if there's something there we can turn it into a formal project and communicate to employees" won't fly under General Data Protection Regulation (GDPR), for instance.

Here is a list of questions you ought to be able to answer before getting your hands on the network data:

1. What are the questions you are aiming to answer?
2. Why are there no alternative ways of answering these questions?
3. Where is the limit? What data will you not use?
4. Who does the analysis of such data benefit and in what ways?
5. Who might the analysis of such data harm? How will you mitigate such harm?

As an example, let's say we want to understand whether Gen Z new hires are getting as much one-on-one time with their manager as new hires of other generations because the survey results found this segment to be the least engaged. How would you answer the questions above? Let's practice:

- What are the questions you are aiming to answer?
  - How much time do employees who have been with the company for less than three months get with their managers?
  - How does this amount of time differ across generations?
  - Why are there no alternative ways of answering these questions?

While it is possible to ask employees to self-report on the time spent with their manager or team members, if we want to use more than a week worth of data, we'd be relying on the employees' memory, which may be biased or inaccurate.

- Where is the limit? What data will you not use? We will use actual time spent in meetings rather than just the invite sent and accepted since accepted meetings may go over or sometimes not actually happen. We will not use the transcript of meeting data even if it's available as it is not relevant for the question and is too intrusive.
- Who does the analysis of such data benefit and in what ways? New hires and managers who might need to understand the importance of one-on-one time. The analysis can provide guidance on the optimal amount of one-on-one time, as too much

time can also be a sign of micromanaging rather than productive one-on-one discussion.

- Who might the analysis of such data harm? How will you mitigate such harm?
  - Managers who are not spending appropriate time with their team or are showing bias in how they spend time with different team members
  - Employees who don't want their data used for this analysis

For managers, we will start by having conversations with the stakeholders responsible for manager effectiveness in our organization. We can work together to ensure the data analysis is going to be used for development purposes only and will not impact compensation or promotion decisions. This can give managers time to change how they lead the team.

For employees this is a difficult one to mitigate. Communication is key. We will communication exactly how the data will be used and how it will not be used. One other potential mitigation is to provide an opportunity to opt out of the analysis.

Additional questions around DEI and well-being that are perfect for passive data to answer include the following:

- Do individuals who look like each other invite those who don't look like them into a conversation?
- Are managers more likely to promote those who look like them?
- Are the optional happy hours really optional and are they inclusive?
- Are women and people of color over mentored and under sponsored?
- Are Gen Z and millennials more likely to struggle with unplugging than other generations?
- Do new hires work more from the office?
- Do employees who get more face time with senior leaders get promoted faster?
- Does the majority group interrupt the minority group more in a meeting?

- Do employees who work in different time zones experience longer work hours?
- Are women or men more likely to get credit for their ideas in a meeting?

While there may be external research covering these topics, none uses feedback and data from your current employees. It'll be difficult to convince stakeholders with data that aren't representative of your organization.

Let's take a few of these questions and form an analysis.

- Are Gen Z and millennials more likely to struggle with unplugging? What data would you need?

You'll need to be able to define "unplugging" first. Does it mean checking mail or having chat and meetings outside normal business hours? Does it mean doing so while on paid time off (PTO)?

If it is work outside "normal business hours," how will you define it for everyone and will it be accurate at all times? If you work on a distributed team, you know that collaborating across time zones can be a challenge. Daylight saving time in the United States poses another challenge where some months and states are on a different time zone. Defining business hours the same for everyone can result in mislabeling someone's work in the evening as an "inability to unplug" while the team might have agreed to slightly different working hours for collaboration purposes. I recall starting and ending my day later when most of my team was on the west coast, for instance. Now, of course, there is limit to this shift in work hours, since working 10 p.m.–6 a.m. daily to collaborate with colleagues on the other side of the world isn't a sustainable practice.

If this isn't complicated enough, consider what happens when some of the employees on this team travel. What do normal business hours mean while they are on the road? Is it the local time of their destination? Is it the same as their home because that's what their body clock is used to? There isn't an absolutely correct answer. It requires some initial analysis to understand how big a problem this is in the first place. If only a very small group of employees travel and it's a major part of their job, or if travel only occurs infrequently for employees, it isn't as much of an issue. It would be complex to measure "ability to unplug" consistently and accurately for everyone all the time, so you'll want to focus on the big picture instead.

From a data perspective, travel or work location of the day isn't the easiest or cleanest data to use. PTO often sits in another system. When I work with these types of data, I know perfection is impossible and strive for *good enough* to answer the key questions.

- Do employees who get more face time with senior leaders get promoted faster?

Dell surprised its employees and the world with an announcement that remote workers wouldn't be eligible for promotions in 2024. This was a sharp contrast to the company's stance in 2022, when Dell's chief described the company as "committed to allow team members around the globe to choose the work style that best fit their lifestyle—whether that is remote or in an office or a blend of the two."[11]

I started running analysis to see if there's a gap in pay and promotion between employees working in the office and those who were remote long before the COVID-19 pandemic. In some teams, I'd observed a difference in promotions while there is no gap in other teams. Prior to the pandemic, this quick analysis gave us information on the hypothesis that "you must be in the office to be promoted." After the pandemic, this same analysis gave us insights into how managers are handling the fluid work situations as we navigated return-to-office decisions.

The quickest way to set up the analysis is to compare employees by remote status. If you want to get more precise, you can see if additional data on the number of days in-office is available so you can see if there is a correlation between in-office time and promotions and if there is a "sweet spot."

- Are women or men more likely to get credit for their ideas in a meeting?

A 2017 research on US professionals finds that men are given more credit than women even when saying the same thing.[12] The phenomenon of a woman's idea being repeated by men in meetings is so pervasive that it has a name "hepeating" in popular culture.

When does this issue matter? While some may argue this is a simple annoyance and doesn't impact business results, imagine you are in a success planning or talent discussion. The question around creative problem solvers comes up. Whose name will you remember? Likely the people who speak up and get credit for their ideas. Even if there are no bad intentions, the individuals who don't receive credit may never make it to the list of "top talent" and receive the promotions for which they are qualified.

For accurate data, you'd need an add-on to capture context in virtual meetings. The contextual questions, like who took credit for someone else's idea are challenging to answer without full analysis of the entire meeting conversation. This will be time-consuming and costly unless you have a tool that analyzes meeting content for you.

Face-to-face Communication Data

Network analysis based on email and chat data can only capture digital interactions. What about face-to-face interactions? Humanyze, a people analytics software provider, has deployed sociometric badges that employees wear to capture conversations in the office. The study finds that face-to-face communication is associated with better performance when working on difficult projects. Their 2008 research on a group of IT employees shows that "more face-to-face communication is positively correlated with productivity; meanwhile, more email communication leads to less productivity."[13]

Now that we have covered both active and passive data, let's talk about something less sexy but important—data governance, specifically, data access.

Regardless of how the data were gathered, you'll have to answer a critical question: Who should have access to the DEI and well-being data in an organization? This is not a compliance conversation but a strategic one. I recall several conversations with the chief human resources officer (CHRO) and ERG leaders where there is a debate between whether ERG leaders should have access to "HR data." The CHRO is often concerned about DEI and well-being data ending up in the wrong hands and possibly leaked to the media. On the other hand, ERG leaders often push for transparency and accountability. Both sides are right, so what should you do? The perception in many organizations is that HR data are special and should be treated as such. I've found it easier to have the governance conversation with those responsible for enterprise data strategy than keeping the conversation within HR. One of the reasons being, ultimately, HR data are part of enterprise data. The governance philosophy and successful implementation require the support of the enterprise data team, including data engineering, security, and privacy setup.

Table 1.1 shows a sample data access worksheet you can bring to a conversation with the data strategy team, and as usual, the decisions should be consulted with privacy and legal teams.

Table 1.1 Sample Data Access Worksheet

	External to company	Internal – SLT	Internal – Managers	Internal – DEI leadership team	Internal – ERG leaders	Internal – HR leaders	Internal – Data teams
Aggregate DEI and well-being data							
Individual level DEI and well-being data							

There is rarely any justification for individual level data given the sensitivity. When it comes to well-being related metrics in particular, you could get into private health information (PHI) that is governed differently than regular employee data.

In the survey discussion earlier, we mentioned the complexity of gathering text data. If someone discloses their medical conditions in a survey, how will such data be stored and protected? Who will be able to see such information? If the passive data collected revealed harassment based on someone's medical condition, how will such data be stored and protected? This is an unlikely scenario but should be aligned with stakeholders beforehand.

While quantitative data are important, it is not the only data we can use to measure DEI and well-being. That's where qualitative data comes in. The next section explores the role of qualitative data in depth and how you can leverage both types of data together effectively.

Qualitative Data: Focus Groups and In-depth Interviews

How do you gather qualitative data outside of survey comments? Focus groups and interviews are another common approach to getting such data.

When do you use focus groups as opposed to survey comments? There are a few situations when a focus group is more appropriate. First, is when the issues are too sensitive to write about in the comments. Second, is when there is not enough psychological safety for employees to speak up. Third, is when focus groups are needed as a follow-up to surveys for a deep dive.

Can you do focus groups online or without video? Yes. Bulletin board focus groups can be another option where the moderator provides questions and allows respondents to reflect before responding. This asynchronous discussion can be an alternative when time zones are a challenge or when the video interview mode is not suitable for everyone participating. For this to be successful, it is important to have clear rules around what is appropriate to share and what might be off limits. The privacy considerations should be clarified beforehand as well. No screenshots or pictures of what is mentioned in these groups should be permitted, for instance.

What Exactly Is a Focus Group?

Ernest Dichter, a marketing and psychological expert, coined the name "focus group" in 1991. This term describes meetings held with a small group of participants who gather to discuss and share openly on a particular topic.

The hosting organization carefully selects participants for the study to represent the larger population they're attempting to target.

The right group members affect the results of your research, so it's vital to be thoughtful when selecting members.

Roles

There are two roles in a focus group: moderator and participant.

The moderator asks questions and facilitates the sharing within the group. One of the most important goals is to ensure the research is not biased and can be generalized to the entire company's opinions.

The participants, consisting of a group of 6 to 10 people, share their opinions, knowledge, and feedback openly during the focus group.

Questions to Ask During the Participant Selection Process

To ensure you have participants representing different parts of the business, it is helpful to ask a few questions during the participant selection process. Following are examples of the types of questions you can include.

1. Please indicate how long you have worked in _____ (company or business unit name).
   • Under 1 year
   • 1–5 years

- 6–10 years
- 10+ years
2. Please indicate your work location.
   - New York City
   - San Francisco
   - Chicago
   - Atlanta
   - Houston
3. Please indicate your age range.
   - Under 30
   - 30–39
   - 40–49
   - 50–59
   - 60+
   - Prefer not to answer
4. Please indicate your gender
   - Female
   - Male
   - Non-binary
   - Prefer not to answer

These are four common segments for illustrative purposes. You can add additional demographic questions to help segment the participants to understand how their feedback differs across these groups. For instance, you can choose generation instead of age group or opt for adding race/ethnicity as you see fit.

A Simple Framework for Questions to Ask During a Focus Group

You can open the focus group with open questions, then dive deeper into the impact of the issue on an important key performance indicator (KPI) such as retention, and close with an open ended "what else?" Here is a flexible framework I have used and you can tailor to structure the discussion.

1. What are your thoughts about _____ (issue)?
2. How does the _____ (issue) affect your willingness to recommend our company to your friends?

3. What are we doing well on this _____ (issue) currently?
4. Where can we improve on this _____ (issue)?
5. Is there anything we haven't discussed that you'd like to add? (Closing)

In a DEI and well-being focus group, here are some specific questions you can ask.

1. Are there places/times at work where you experience feelings of belonging or inclusion?
2. Are there places/times at work that you feel excluded or that you don't belong?
3. How would you describe your first impression of our company's diversity, equity, and inclusion?
4. Has your impression changed in any way, and if so, how?
5. How does our leadership commitment to DEI affect your intent to stay at our company?
6. How is our company doing on promoting the well-being of employees?
7. Are there times when you feel worried about having enough time to get all the work done?
8. What does your manager say or do to let you know they care about your well-being?

You'll need to tailor the language for the participants.

Here are simple guidelines for creating good questions for your focus group:

- Have language that resonates with all participants.
- Each question covers one topic rather than multiple.
- Create a welcoming environment for open discussion.

A few questions to ask yourself as you draft questions for the focus group:

- Are the employees used to more formal or informal language?
- Are there any corporate jargons we should avoid?

- Is the language inclusive and understandable to everyone invited?

To be inclusive, I'd also recommend sending out the agenda and questions beforehand. For neurodivergent and nonnative-speaker employees, it can be an overwhelming experience without clarity.

The Pros and Cons of Focus Groups

Should you collect your opinions from groups or from individuals? If designed with diverse participants, a key advantage of focus groups is depth and variety of perspectives. Additionally, focus group participants can often stimulate new thoughts for each other, which would not occur on an individual basis.

There can be downsides as well. Depending on the topic, certain group members might feel hesitant about speaking openly. Finding time that works for a group can also be challenging and cause delays in the data gathering process.

If you know group discussions will not be productive for the specific topic, consider the alternative of conducting individual interviews.

Individual Interviews

These can be more intimate and in-depth conversations. If the interviewees are uncomfortable sharing in front of others due to the nature of the topic, it is more productive to have individual interviews. Imagine if a particular leader is described as unethical; the group conversation may not allow individuals to speak up freely. Are there downsides to using individual interviews instead of focus groups? Not many, assuming time isn't an issue. One downside of individual interviews is that hiring external consultants can be costly.

The Role of External Facilitators

A tech company had created an initiative to increase representation of women in tech. After years of making little progress and hearing some noises around the work environment, the HR team hired an external consultant to meet with women individually about their work experience.

Why didn't they use an internal facilitator? They were interested in the truth, however difficult it might be to hear. They were concerned that an internal facilitator would share the same network as some of the interviewees, so they may not feel 100% comfortable opening up about issues with colleagues or leaders at work.

The series of interviews uncovered issues with a few senior leaders' management approaches. The HR team then provided coaching to these leaders. This is an example of when it's helpful to have individual interviews.

Text Analytics

Every year I'd run into C-level executives telling me proudly they'd read every single comment on their employee survey. Then without fail, they'd immediately ask me to analyze the comments and come up with a recommendation. Why? Human brains simply aren't as good as machines at processing and synthesizing thousands of text comments. I've witnessed the maturity of text analytics in survey vendors as well as internal analytics teams from simple word clouds in early days to analyzing the sentiment around specific topics. We have made much progress in improving our understanding of employee comments without having to read every single comment.

How do you turn thousands of comments into actionable insights and recommendations? We can do that in five steps of analysis:

Themes and Keywords

Imagine if you have to fill in the blanks in your presentation summarizing the comments: *overall, our employees are most concerned about* _____, _____, *and* _____.

Think of the purpose of the overall themes and keywords analysis as the overview you can share with the CEO about the current employee sentiment. I recommend keeping the overview succinct as your CEO will want quick takeaway as soon as the survey results are out. In large organizations and public companies in particular, the employee sentiment is a regular pulse on the health of the organization. The leadership team often shares high level results with the board of directors on a regular basis.

Sentiment Around Themes and Keywords

The second helpful analysis is to understand the sentiment around each of the key themes and keywords. Whether the sentiment is positive, negative, neutral, or mixed, tell us additional information about the particular theme.

For instance, "collaboration" often comes up as a theme in employee survey comments, but is it described with a negative or positive sentiment? To understand the context, I suggest looking at several comments with that theme highlighted. If employees describe collaboration with a positive sentiment, these comments can offer details on the specific part of the collaboration that is working well or a particular technology that has enabled collaboration.

On the other hand, if employees describe collaboration with a negative sentiment, exploring the comments can tell you what the barriers to collaboration are.

Segment by Favorable Versus Not

A simple yet powerful way to understand comments is to combine text and quantitative answers in a single analysis. Do those who responded favorably to "I am included in discussions around important decisions at work" comment differently than those who responded unfavorably to the same question? They likely do. You'd expect the overall sentiment to be more positive in the comments of those who responded favorably. However, what are the themes in these segments of employees? Are there concrete recommendations you can make from these themes?

For illustrative purposes, Figure 1.3 provides an example of how this type of segmentation can offer additional context and insights beyond quantitative scores. By excluding the neutral responses, this analysis highlights problem areas for improvement, such as "meetings" and "waiting." Reviewing the full comments can provide the missing context for one-word phrases like "remote" or "team," which shows up as a key theme for both survey participants who selected unfavorable and favorable responses.

One way to think about these is "what's going well" versus "what's problematic." While it's possible you'll encounter suggestions that are impractical to implement, splitting the text by favorable and unfavorable gives you a quick overview of what's working and what's not.

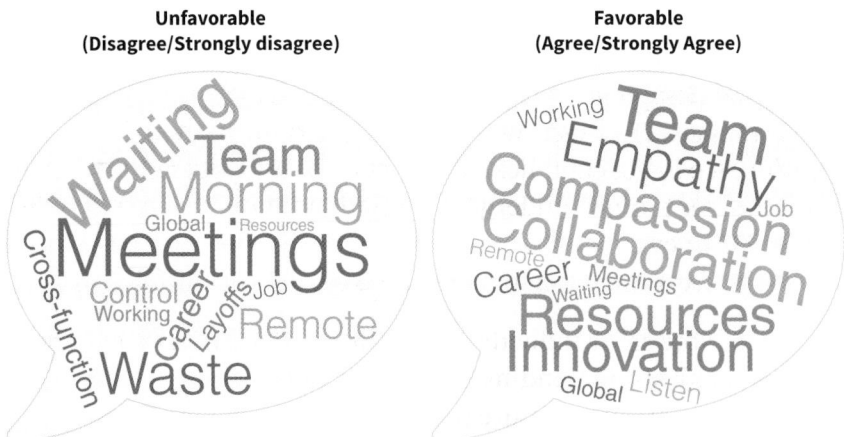

Figure 1.3 Text Analytics Example of Segmentation by Favorable vs. Unfavorable Responses

Segment by Groups of Employees

How are different groups of employees feeling about the various aspects of work?

Is the sentiment around key themes different by tenure, function, and location?

A note on analysis paralysis. You'll likely have too many filters than too few to slice and dice the survey data. Focus on specific questions your stakeholders care about and are actionable before you start this exercise.

Trending Analysis of Comments

Be prepared to answer some key questions with the analysis:

- What changed since the last time they took the survey?
- Did the top themes change from the last time?
- For the repeated themes, how did the sentiment change since last time?

Some survey software will provide this type of trending analysis out of the box, and if you don't have such access, it'll require a comparison analysis of the comments from two surveys.

At the company level, it may not be too difficult to compare broad themes. However, within each function, business unit, and location, it can get complicated especially when organizations look very different after undergoing rapid growth or restructuring between surveys.

There are a few ways to make the comparison more reliable:

1. Limit to the same individuals who were in both surveys in the trend analysis. Depending on the response rate and survey setup, this may be an unrealistic approach if the resulting respondents are too low or it is not technically feasible.
2. Limit to the groups that did not experience a drastic change in employees. For example, if the pizza business unit was recently

acquired, consider excluding it for the analysis given none of these employees were present in the prior survey.

In the data world, longitudinal data are considered a goldmine. If you have team or individual level data, you can conclude with more confidence in describing a trend. In other words, you'd know a particular change occurred in the same group of individuals and isn't simply a result of a different group of people responding to the survey. When it comes to comments, however, because not everyone who responded to the survey will take the survey again and not everyone who responds comments, this may result in a too restricted set of comments to analyze.

I recommend doing an analysis of both sets of data and seeing if the trends differ drastically. Specifically, perform the trends analysis to show what changed from the last survey while acknowledging some of the changes observed might be due to respondents being different. Then restrict the data to exclude individuals or groups that are deemed incomparable, such as a newly acquired business unit, to show what has changed for previous employees. By doing both, you can offer more detailed insights, including whether certain company programs that were created based on feedback in the prior survey have changed employees' perceptions this time around.

Note that while this section focuses on survey comments, you can apply the same method to the notes gathered from focus groups and interviews. Some organizations repeat similar focus groups on DEI and well-being topics on a regular basis so these text data can be analyzed in similar ways as those gathered on a survey.

Text Analytics

During the beginning of the pandemic, a tech company surveyed its employees every two weeks on health and well-being related topics to keep a pulse on them. One word that repeated frequently in the survey text comments was "chair." Upon closer examination, the analytics team realized it's related to the discomfort of their chair while working from home. A new benefit was created to reimburse employees for office chair purchases. It was a few hundred dollars per employee that made the comment go away pretty immediately and improved the sentiment as a result. This is an example of concrete and fast actions that an employer took based on listening to the employees' feedback.

The Role of AI

Since ChatGPT took over the world like a storm, I frequently receive questions around what generative AI (GenAI) can do in the world of employee experience measurement.

Imagine having a super-smart assistant who can read through all your survey comments in seconds, understanding not just the words, but the meaning behind them. That's essentially what GenAI can do for your organization. Tools like ChatGPT, Gemini, and Claude can automatically sort comments into themes, letting you quickly see what topics are on your employees' minds.

For instance, you might find that "work-life balance" is mentioned in 50% of comments, while "compensation" comes up in 20%. This gives you a snapshot of what matters to your workforce.

Additionally, GenAI tools can detect the tone of comments. They can tell you if people are expressing frustration or excitement about different aspects of their experience. This emotional context is crucial for truly understanding the respondents' perspectives and creating an action plan to address the corresponding pain points.

Moreover, these tools can quickly identify when employees are making suggestions or highlighting problems that need attention. Imagine being able to filter for all the constructive suggestions about improving "manager effectiveness" across different departments. That's the kind of targeted insight these systems can provide rapidly, without hours of manual reading and analysis.

The best part of these AI-powered tools and the reason they became popular quickly is that you don't need to be an expert to use them. Most tools are designed to be user-friendly, allowing anyone to ask questions in plain language and quickly receive clear insights.

For example, you could ask, "What are the main concerns of our European sales team regarding the CRM system?" The AI assistant would then sort through relevant comments, summarize the key points, and suggest potential solutions based on the feedback.

This technology can also allow for more sophisticated analysis. You could compare and contrast the sentiments of different functions, locations, age groups, or tenure levels on specific issues. Such analysis can help you spot trends or issues before they become major problems. By analyzing comment patterns over time, they can alert you to growing concerns or shifting priorities among your workforce. Was "work-life balance" always mentioned in 50% of the comments? Was there a time when it was a minor concern? What changed? To show the results to your stakeholders, you can even create dashboards with a line of prompt.

While GenAI tools are powerful, it's important to remember that they're still only meant to act as your copilot so the insights should augment, not replace, human judgment. The information they provide should be a useful starting point for deeper discussions and strategic planning. With the help of GenAI, we can make more informed decisions and respond more quickly to employee needs.

In this chapter, we discussed how to measure DEI and well-being, with both quantitative and qualitative data, and ended with how GenAI could serve as the copilot in your analysis. The next chapter will cover people data storytelling, which is key to influencing your stakeholders to take action to create an inclusive and healthy work environment where all employees can thrive.

Notes

1. Google. (2023). *Diversity annual report—Google diversity equity & inclusion* [online]. Google. Available at: https://about.google/belonging/diversity-annual-report/2023/

2. Source: Mock data created by the author.

3. McKinsey. (2022). *Women in the workplace archive reports (2015–2022)* [online]. McKinsey. Available at: https://www.mckinsey.com/featured-insights/diversity-and-inclusion/women-in-the-workplace-archive

4. Field, E., Krivkovich, A., Kügele, S., Robinson, N., and Yee, L. (2024). *Women in the workplace.* McKinsey. Available at: https://www.mckinsey.com/featured-insights/diversity-and-inclusion/women-in-the-workplace

5. Somers, M. (2022). *Women are less likely than men to be promoted. Here's one reason why* [online]. MIT Sloan. Available at: https://mitsloan.mit.edu/ideas-made-to-matter/women-are-less-likely-men-to-be-promoted-heres-one-reason-why

6. Sull, D. and Sull, C. (2023). The toxic culture gap shows companies are failing women. *MIT Sloan Management Review.* Available at: https://sloanreview.mit.edu/article/the-toxic-culture-gap-shows-companies-are-failing-women/

7. Edmondson, A.C. (1996). Learning from mistakes is easier said than done: Group and organizational influences on the detection and correction of human error. *Journal of Applied Behavioral Science* 32(1), 5–28. https://doi.org/10.1177/0021886396321001

8. Martins, L.L., Schilpzand, M.C., Kirkman, B.L., Ivanaj, S., and Ivanaj, V. (2013). A contingency view of the effects of cognitive diversity on team performance: The moderating roles of team psychological safety and relationship conflict. *Small Group Research* 44(2), 96–126. https://doi.org/10.1177/1046496412466921

9. Author's conversation with Andrew Pitts, founder and CEO of Polinode, a provider of organizational network analysis solutions.

10. Kost, D. (2020). *You're right! You are working longer and attending more meetings* [online]. Harvard Business School Working Knowledge. Available at: https://hbswk.hbs.edu/item/you-re-right-you-are-working-longer-and-attending-more-meetings

11. Harding, S. (2024). Dell tells remote workers that they won't be eligible for promotion [online]. Ars Technica. Available at: https://arstechnica.com/information-technology/2024/03/dell-tells-remote-workers-that-they-wont-be-eligible-for-promotion/

12. ScienceDaily. (2017). *Women get less credit than men in the workplace* [online]. Available at: https://www.sciencedaily.com/releases/2017/12/171213130252.htm

13. Wu, L., Waber, B.N., Aral, S., Brynjolfsson, E., and Pentland, A. (2008). Mining face-to-face interaction networks using sociometric badges: Predicting productivity in an IT configuration task. *SSRN Electronic Journal.* doi:https://doi.org/10.2139/ssrn.1130251

Chapter 2
People Data Storytelling

To inspire action, your data story must be clear, your audience must care, and there has to be a call to action!

– Dr. Serena Huang

What do you think of when you hear "Data Storytelling"? Charts and presentations? Interactive dashboards? My definition of **Data Storytelling** goes beyond these traditional realms. Successful data storytelling enables you to inspire action from your stakeholders. It is to communicate recommendations and insights from data using visualizations and narratives.

Why People Data Storytelling Is Different

If you have worked with people data, you know that they are indeed special. And because they are special, it makes the storytelling more challenging.

The privacy and sensitivity, in particular, means that strangely, you might not always know who has the correct and up-to-date data in the organization. In most HR organizations, some are so data sensitive that almost no one has access to it. Think about the list of employees who are to be laid off, or the ones who are on a performance-improvement plan (PIP). Even with job openings, there may be confidential searches that are not visible to everyone due to upcoming restructuring. These super sensitive data are at best, securely locked away in part of the people data warehouse, and at worst, are in a password protected spreadsheet on someone's laptop. In the real world of HR, there is often data that have to be offline before public announcement of big changes.

Another aspect that is unique is the emotional connection. People or employee data are, by nature, personal and emotional. This is a double-edged sword for storytelling. You must be mindful of the emotional impact the narrative may have. It may be easy to find data points that evoke strong emotions in the audience.

Furthermore, human behaviors are complex and can be difficult to quantify. A lot of information about employees aren't observed and captured.

If this isn't complex enough, there are always multiple stakeholders in people data projects, including employees, managers, HR teams, and executives. Storytellers must consider the diverse needs and perspectives of these stakeholders when crafting their narrative.

To overcome these challenges, I've found it helpful to do the following:

- Collaborate with HR and employee data experts to ensure accuracy and credibility
- Use storytelling and visualization to convey complex data insights
- Provide recommendations and narratives that are actionable

The Role of Trust

The lack of trust in people data can be an uphill battle in any organization. If your stakeholders doubt the accuracy of data whenever you present an analysis, it might be time to first focus on the quality and governance of data. Early in my career, I underestimated the importance of trust in analytics projects. I found myself in a few presentations that weren't productive because we couldn't stop arguing over the accuracy of data presented on a page.

When I first arrive in an organization, I always sit down with stakeholders and ask, "How good is your HR data?" When I ask HR leaders, some would quantify it for me while others would provide a long explanation of why it's not as good as it should be. When I ask the IT organization on the other hand, I'd often get different answers. Typically, IT would give me metrics around data quality or how close to real time the data in the system are. IT also tends to tell me a more positive answer than HR. Why? It's because the perspectives are different. How IT and HR use employee data isn't the same. The third group I talk to is the managers with large teams and who have access to the employee data. This is often the most interesting: where some managers were surprised to find out they had any access at all, others might have created their own database over time because they believe it's more accurate than what is in the HR system. For instance, there are sometimes issues with the termination dates and termination reasons data. Managers may have the most up-to-date information on their employees and this is not corrected and reflected in the HR system.

When Data Quality Meets AI

AI has taken over the corporate world since the release of ChatGPT. My colleagues who are chief data officers have been under pressure to use AI and felt their data quality or infrastructure wasn't ready for the full power of AI. I've been there, too. I'd say our data quality needed to be fixed before running predictive analytics or any AI or machine learning models. My stakeholders would not take me seriously for the longest time, until I shared a real-life example of what happened when I utilized poor quality data in building a model.

I discovered a strange pattern when building a predictive employee attrition model. It was doing an okay job predicting resignations though it would "accidently" predict those who were about to be dismissed involuntarily as well. I could not figure out why because the attrition prediction model was trained to predict voluntary attrition or resignations and only those historic

(continued)

(continued)

data were included. After lots of analysis, it was discovered that years ago some of the employee attrition was incorrectly labeled, so the training data wasn't restricted to voluntary attrition as I designed it to be! If you didn't think data quality mattered that much, think again.

Once you've confirmed that there is a fundamental level of trust in the data quality, you can work toward telling stories with this data.

The Three Cs Framework for Successful Data Storytelling

There are three Cs that take your storytelling from average to successful: **Clear**, **Care**, and **Call to Action**.

The first C, **Clear**, is where the data story is self-explanatory so you don't need to explain the chart or presentation. As the head of analytics, I used to have a simple rule for my team that if the recipient of our presentation asks us to explain the chart, then the data story was not clear enough.

Imagine you're presenting a complex report to a group of senior executives. You don't want to lose them in a sea of spreadsheets and busy charts. Clarity is about simplifying the complex and presenting it in a way that speaks to your audience. Here are some tips to ensure your data story is clear:

1. **Visualize the data story:** Charts, graphs, or infographics are all powerful ways to make data more understandable. A well-designed visual can convey information in a way that's memorable to your stakeholders.
2. **Keep the language simple:** Avoid technical terms, buzz words, and jargons. Make sure the descriptions are understandable to

everyone, even those without prior knowledge of your topic. Don't overwhelm your audience with too many words on the charts and focus on the actionable insights.

3. **Label appropriately:** Your data story needs to be clearly labeled so the audience knows instantly what each axis, line, bar, and color represent.

Clear

Being "clear" isn't only about making data understandable, it's about speeding up the data-to-action cycle. When data are presented clearly, they can:

- **Build Trust:** A clear data story builds trust between the presenter and the audience. It shows that you're not just throwing numbers at them; you've carefully analyzed the data, and you're sharing the most important information with them.
- **Increase Engagement:** When people understand what is in front of them, they're more likely to engage with it and remember the key insights.
- **Drive Action:** Most importantly, clear data insights can inspire people to take action, whether it's adopting a new strategy, changing a behavior, or making a decision. Think about the last time you were asked to take action on what you didn't understand. Were you reluctant to do so?

"Clear" is the foundation upon which all other elements of effective storytelling are built. Without clarity, your data will remain unseen and unused. So, every time you're presenting data, remember to ask yourself: Is this clear?

Let's walk through some examples.

Which of these two graphs in Figure 2.1 is **clearer**?

The graph on the bottom is much easier to read. The bars are clearly labeled and the 2D versus 3D nature is easier on the eyes as well.

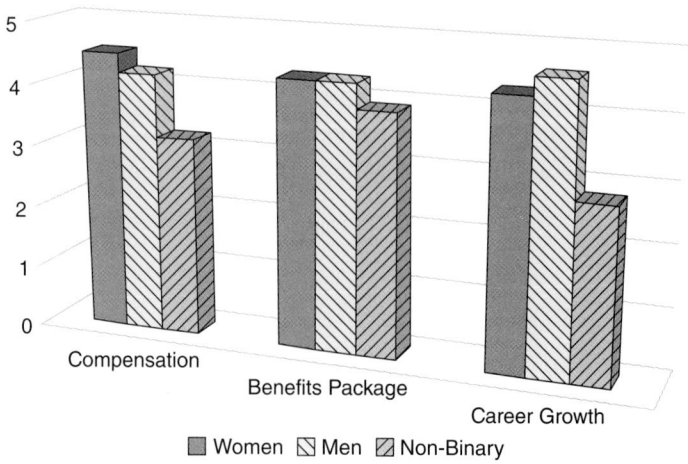

Satisfaction Level by Gender (0–5)

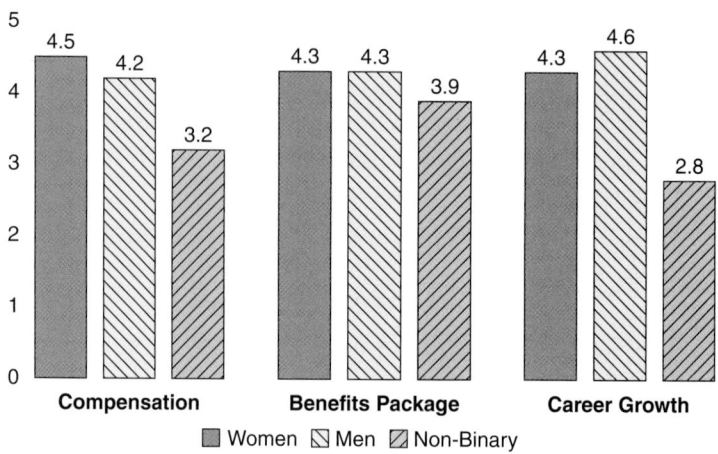

Figure 2.1   Satisfaction Level by Gender

What about these two graphs in Figure 2.2? Both are showing the number of employees across regions.

The top graph is clear in terms of numbers, but it is potentially more helpful to see how the distribution compares across regions. In bottom graph, you can see clearly that south and non-US regions

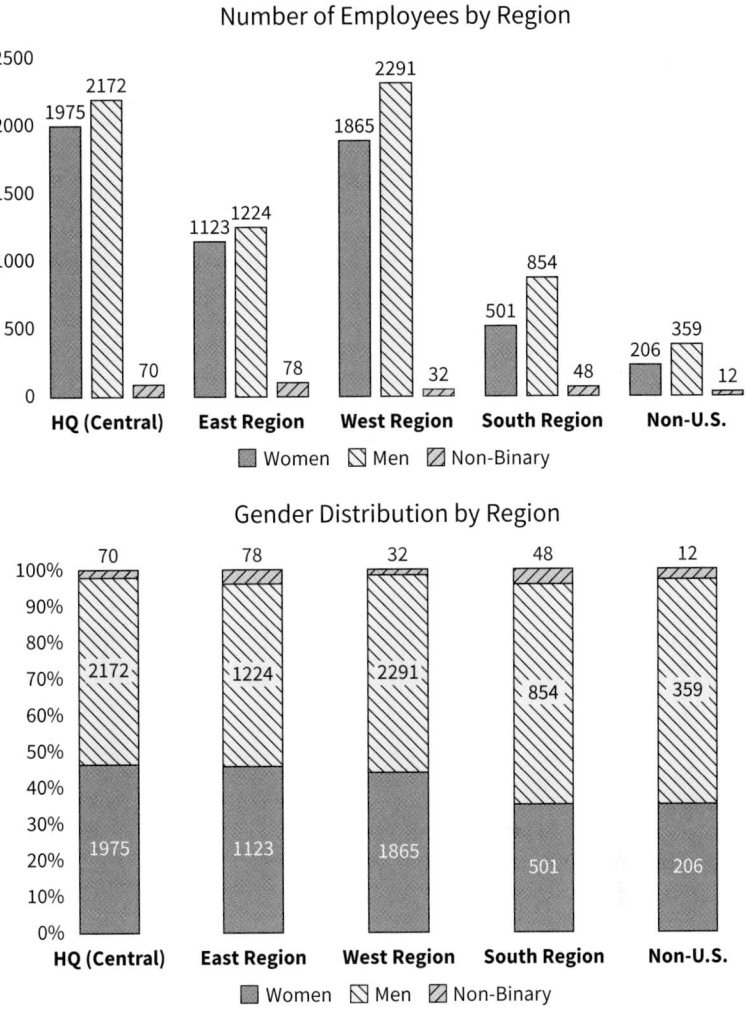

Figure 2.2   Gender Distribution by Region

have the lowest percentage of women. Alternative labels of percentage can be added to the chart to make this clearer. It really depends on what question your audience is looking to answer, which takes us to the next "C," **Care**.

Care

You audience must care about your story. I'll never forget the first time I hired a data scientist on my team. I was so excited to have another technical mind join the team and we whiteboarded all the possibilities with advanced analytics. We proceeded to make one of the ideas come alive and created a model highly predictive of employee attrition. I walked into an HR executive's office and proudly shared with her that I had a model that predicted attrition with 98% accuracy. She said to me, "That's great, Serena. How wonderful. But the attrition rate in my business unit has stayed flat at 2% over the past five years. What really keeps me up at night is the fact that 80% of the senior leaders are retirement eligible next year and I don't have a succession plan. Can your model help with that?"

This experience taught me a valuable lesson: **never solve a problem your stakeholders don't care about.** To understand their short- and long-term priorities, engage them in meaningful conversations. Here are some questions I recommend you ask your stakeholders during the annual strategy discussion and follow-up check-ins:

- What are your organization's priorities in the next 12, 24, and 60 months?
- What's a pain point that if solved could accelerate your growth by 2x to 5x?
- What has your organization been needing to do but hasn't had the resources or time to execute?

How often you touch base with your stakeholders will vary depending on the project complexity and organization culture. I'd recommend at minimum a monthly rhythm. If that sounds like a lot, it's only 12 times per year on the calendar, and likely you'll end up with 10 because of some vacation-heavy seasons. Ask yourself: Is that sufficient time for the change you wish to drive?

During a monthly check-in, your focus needs to be tracking progress on short-term goals, identifying any roadblocks, and ensuring alignment with long-term priorities. Here is the suggested agenda for discussion.

- **Progress Update:** "What progress have we made on the top two or three priorities we discussed last month? Are there any roadblocks we need to remove?"
- **Immediate Needs:** "Are there any new immediate challenges that have emerged this month that we should prioritize?"
- **Alignment Check:** "How does the work we're doing this month contribute to the overall goals we discussed in the annual planning session?"

During a quarterly check-in, you'll want to evaluate progress toward longer-term goals, identifying emerging trends, and pivot your strategies as needed.

- **Quarterly Review:** "Looking back at the past quarter, what were the top three achievements? What were the biggest challenges?"
- **Emerging Trends:** "What new trends or opportunities have emerged in the past quarter that we should consider for our future plans?"
- **Strategic Realignment:** "Considering the progress we've made and the emerging trends, are there any adjustments we need to make to our strategic priorities for the next quarter?"
- **Resource Allocation:** "Are there any changes in resource allocation needed based on the performance and priorities we've discussed?"
- **Team Feedback:** "How did our team's work contribute to your overall goals this quarter? Are there areas where our team could have provided more value or better met your objectives this quarter?"

Notice how *none* of these questions directly ask about data? That's by design. In these stakeholder meetings, you want to think of the discussions as two-way strategic conversations. You can hold yourself accountable by sharing a summary after each check-in with everyone in the meeting. The agreed-upon tasks should go into your project management or planning software immediately with clear deadlines. In general, I've found **active listening** and **being transparent** helpful in keeping the check-ins productive for both the stakeholders and my team.

One of my mentors told me that to be a successful consultant, you have to be able to hear "what's unsaid." I thought it was the most ridiculous advice at first, until I understood what they meant. In these check-ins, pay attention to the body language and facial expressions of your stakeholders. If what they are saying doesn't match what they seem to be feeling, it's time to gently dig deeper. If you can figure out the unsaid, you have a chance to help them with their real needs.

Why is being transparent particularly important in stakeholder conversations? One thing you can count on with data is that data are messy. Everything takes longer than you hoped. The data quality is rarely as good as you hoped. If there are data issues that can impact the timeline on any deliverables, you want to clarify expectations in these conversations. If you run into a snag with the machine learning model and the results are unexpected, you'll want to bring it up candidly. I understand it can be nerve-racking to discuss issues with your stakeholders, and I also remember I was always relieved after the conversation and the issues were all solvable. When you bring your stakeholders into these difficult conversations early on, you are asking them to join you on the journey and co-create the solution.

The Role of Attention

Before you get your audience to care, you must have their attention. One way to get your audience's attention is to evoke emotions. Our brains are wired to listen to stories, so I often encourage data professionals to invest in learning to tell stories with data early on.

"Stories are remembered up to 22 times more than facts alone," said Jennifer Aaker, behavioral scientist and General Atlantic

Professor and Coulter Family Fellow at the Stanford Graduate School of Business.

Imagine a captivating story. It pulls you in, makes you feel something, and leaves a lasting impression. This is because stories engage multiple parts of our brains, creating a powerful connection that sticks with us long after the tale is told.

When someone hears a story, their brain lights up in a symphony of activity:

- Wernicke's area: This region is responsible for language comprehension.
- The amygdala: This emotional powerhouse processes the feelings evoked by the story.
- Mirror neurons: These cells enable us to empathize with the characters and their experiences.

When these different parts of the brain work together, the hippocampus—our short-term memory center—is more likely to convert the experience into a long-term memory.

So, instead of presenting your team with a barrage of numbers, consider how you engage their emotions, spark their curiosity, and connect with them on a deeper level.

Framework to Evoke Feeling

Ask yourself these important questions before you start any data storytelling work:

- How do you want your audience to feel after seeing the story?
- What do you want them to think or do after seeing the story?

Have you ever heard a pointless story, either from a keynote speaker on stage or in a Zoom presentation? You wonder what the point of the story was and what you are supposed to do with that, or you impatiently wait for the presenter to get to their point. If this sounds familiar, it's likely that storyteller didn't keep you and the audience in mind when they were creating the presentation. A great storyteller will make you feel like they are talking with *you*. These two questions instantly shift the focus from the storyteller to the audience. Let's take an example from data on an intent-to-stay analysis:

> Your recent engagement survey shows an overall drop in the intent to stay compared to last year, which isn't surprising given earlier layoffs. However, what is more surprising is that your tenured and senior employees have lower intent to stay than junior employees. On top of that, female director+ have the largest YOY drop in intent to stay, compared with their male counterparts and women who are below the director level.

How do you want your audience to feel? Surprised? Shocked? Sad? Worried? Angry? Curious? These are all valid answers and will mean a different story to tell.

What do you want your audience to think or do? Do you want them to think this is a huge problem and create a retention strategy targeting female director+ population? Do you want them to think it's not a big deal and let you monitor the situation? Of course, you shouldn't form this point of view without analysis and preliminary recommendations. Either way, you'll need to tell the story differently to lead to these thoughts and behaviors.

If you want them to feel curious and worried, for instance, you may try a story around the following trending analysis:

> Our intent to stay had been trending up YOY for 4 years coming out of COVID, until this year. We are seeing a drop for the first time since 2020. Given that our average time to fill an open role has increased recently, this means each person leaving our company will take a bigger toll on the employees who remain.

If you want to highlight the female director+ population, you can anticipate one of the questions your audience will have is why the intent-to-stay has dropped. You can slice and dice the data to find which business unit or function is driving this decrease as a starting point. You can also talk with a few female directors and vice presidents to better understand what might make them want to leave. This combination of quantitative and qualitative data would be helpful in drafting a compelling story.

In times of budget cuts, it is critical to highlight why this potential retention issue deserves attention and investment. You can extrapolate the gender representation for the next 3 years with the current intent-to-stay and show a headline of "we will only have one female vice president and seven female directors remaining by 2027."

Remember: it is your job as the storyteller to grab the attention of your audience, and not for them to figure out why they should care.

Now let's practice with an upcoming conversation or presentation you have.

Ask yourself the following questions:

- How do you want your audience to feel after hearing the story?
- What do you want them to think or do after hearing the story?
- What data, visuals, and narrative would support this?

The "How" of Getting the Audience to Care

To write better narratives in your data story, I encourage you to think more like a *journalist* and less like an *analyst*. Your number one job as a data person is to communicate effectively. Journalists are experts at telling stories that captivate attention and keep you engaged. Ever notice the headlines of breaking news? They draw you in, and you want to read more. Even economic news, which is not the most exciting, rarely shows the data in the headline. You might see something like "Consumer Confidence Fell More Than Expected This Month" and that makes you wonder "how much is that?" so you click on the news to read more. Can you make the title of your next presentation more like a news headline and less like a vague description of data? For example, instead of "Average Starting Salary in Finance (2020–2025)," what about rewriting it to be more attention-grabbing, such as "Average Starting Salary in Finance Reaches Historic High in 2025" or Average Starting Salary in Finance Fell for the First Time Since 2020."

Another way to help your audience care is by providing context around the data you are sharing. When we see a number that represents our performance in any way, we automatically want to know if that's good or bad. Getting an A on a test may be great, but if 95% of the class also got an A, you are pretty average. If your department attrition rate is 20% and the company number is 35%, you are a star when it comes to retaining talent. This is a comparative way to add context. You can provide context to data in other ways, including historical, scaled, confirmative, equivalent, and informational. These correspond to some of the most common asks I'd receive from senior stakeholders: benchmarking (comparative), trending (historical), predictions (scaled).[1] This framework also provides an excellent way to prepare for any upcoming presentations. Ask yourself: Are you ready to provide context around all the data points you are presenting to the audience?

Call to Action

The last "C" of the three Cs framework is "Call to action" (CTA)—in other words, "What do you want me to do?" Never leave it to chance or your audience to figure this out.

You'll want to tie this back to the previous C and focus on why your stakeholders should care first. Use that as a starting point to consider actions that will guide you toward solving the problem.

For instance, if you find out there is a strong link between customer experience and employee experience, and the western region is struggling with having the worst customer Net Promoter Score (NPS) and employee engagement scores, what would you recommend as a CTA? Consider identifying the specific areas of employee experience that drive NPS scores, and recommend ways to improve it supported by analysis.

Storytelling for C-level Executives

I remember a fireside chat I had with a C-level executive who sat through presentations daily, and I asked him what the criteria were for considering recommendations. He said, "The recommendation should answer two questions: Why me and why now?" It was the simplest and most insightful answer I've heard after working in corporate America for 10 years. Does your recommendation address these questions for the stakeholders?

To address the "why me," you must know you are working on what your stakeholders care about.

To address "why now," you have to combine having a clear story with the right call to action. Overall, you need to understand how decisions are made in your business. Is it a single stakeholder who can call the shots?

What does a good call to action look like in DEI and well-being issues? Following are some examples:

- In a data story about employee engagement, you might present data showing that employees who receive useful feedback and discuss career development with their managers have higher levels of intent-to-stay. Your CTA could be to encourage managers to provide regular feedback to their team members during weekly or monthly check-ins.
- In a data story about employee well-being, you might present data showing that remote workers are more likely to experience feelings of isolation and loneliness. Your CTA could be to encourage targeted communication on mental health support and virtual social connection opportunities for remote employees.

Alternatively, you might present data showing that employees on teams where the leader isn't sending after-hours emails and chats are less likely to experience burnout. Your CTA could be to encourage leaders to be role models and set stronger boundaries around work hours. It can be helpful to include specific findings from your data analysis, such as the "tipping point" for when after-hours emails become too much and can lead to burnout or employee turnover.

- In a data story about diversity and inclusion, you might present data showing that employees on teams of managers who receive a particular training are more likely to feel included and valued. Your CTA could be to advocate for this specific training for all managers, based on the analysis of the impact of various training courses.

The Process: From Raw Data to a Compelling Story

Now that you know the keys to success, here's a step-by-step process to go from data to a compelling story.

1. Analyze the data with the problem in mind.
2. Draft a narrative. Think about the headline, then the subheadline in a breaking news article.
3. Create the visualization of data to complement the narrative.

The first step is to analyze your data with clear business problems in mind. You'll want to focus on the issues that are keeping your stakeholders up at night in this step.

For instance, if your stakeholder leads a business unit with difficulty attracting talent but no problem retaining them, focus your analysis on the hiring process rather than attrition.

One way to be focused and efficient in your data analysis process is to start by forming a problem statement. You can bet on the stakeholders caring about this problem: "How can we attract more qualified candidates for open roles?" If key performance indicators (KPIs) are involved, you can be even more specific and form a clear problem statement like, "How can we attract 30% more qualified candidates in the next quarter for engineering roles?"

Next, ask yourself: What would a good recommendation look like? Put yourself in your stakeholder's shoes. They would likely want to know what's causing talent attraction issues in the first place and how to fix them as quickly as possible. The reason I suggest thinking about recommendations at this stage is twofold: (1) you can use this to narrow down the data you need for analysis; (2) you are making sure you have the appropriate business acumen for making recommendations. If your initial gut response is, "I have no idea what actions would be considered," that's a clear sign you have more research and networking to do.

Now that you have a sense of potential recommendations and solutions, you can then take a look at a couple of sources of data: recruitment process and employer branding data. Ask yourself a few more questions worth answering before diving into the analysis:

1. Where in the recruitment process do we lose candidates and how long is our process taking?
2. How do we compare with competitors in terms of number of applicants per role posted?
3. Does our employer brand need attention? What have candidates and employees said about our process?

Now you are ready to roll up your sleeves and dive into the data.

During the second step, you'll draft the narrative based on what your analysis revealed. Going back to the answers to the questions, you can start by drafting a sentence answering each of the questions:

1. We have lots of unqualified candidates in our recruiting process; 439 out of 3,675 applicants are selected for interviews, and it takes 12 days from application to assessment. It's possible that we lost qualified candidates due to the slow review process.
2. Our company lags behind competitors in applicants received per open role.
3. We have several negative reviews on Glassdoor about our interview process, and our company interview experience is worse than competitor A.

This is a good starting point, and you can revisit to finalize the narrative once you do more analysis and visualization.

Finally, you'll create visualizations to complement the narratives in the third step of the process to go from data to a compelling story.

What visual should we consider for this narrative? The **Recruitment Funnel** is a popular request from stakeholders where you can visually identify any bottlenecks. The chart in Figure 2.3 contains two key pieces of data: how many applicants get to the next stage and how many days on average are they in each stage. You can understand the volume and speed at the same time. Is nine days a lot between the application and recruiter review? Depending on the organization and role, it may be a long time or may be fast. You could do some analysis of past data and see if you were losing a smaller percentage of applicants when the application and recruiter review was shorter, for instance.

The review process appears to screen out the most applicants, from more than 3,000 to only 657 applicants. Is this a healthy number? Confirm if most are rejected due to not meeting the basic qualifications, and see if trending data offers insights on this issue. With the AI tools on the market that apply on the candidates' behalf, many employers are receiving a large influx of applications. You'll

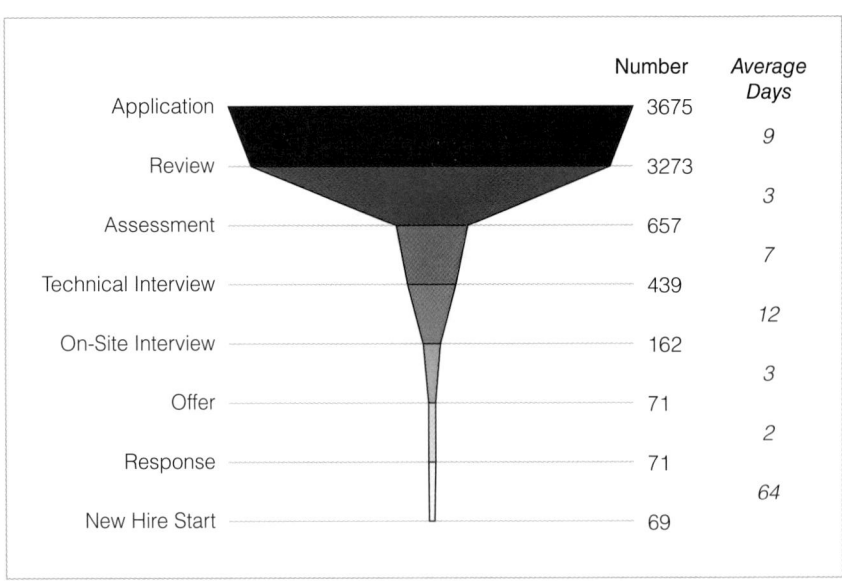

Figure 2.3　Recruitment Funnel

want to monitor the quality of applications as more AI tools continue to emerge.

A note on recruitment funnel charts: A recruitment funnel often has too much detail for most stakeholders. One of the questions I like to ask myself when creating a chart is **whether each bar/ unit/label would provide information so critical that it changes the decision**. If the answer is no, I simplify. You can simplify the chart by combining multiple interview stages, for instance. I also suggest a "side view" of a funnel, as shown in Figure 2.4, which is easier on the eyes and brain.

Now let's look at the answer to question 2, "How do we compare with competitors in terms of number of applicants per role posted?" The data in Figure 2.5 shows our company lags behind competitors in applicants received per open role, though the gap has narrowed recently.

In your deep analysis you can anticipate some of the follow-up questions too:

"Which competitors?"
"How has this changed over time?"
"Are our job posting strategies different than theirs?"

Prepare yourself for these questions if you are going to send or present this chart to your stakeholders. You can have the answers

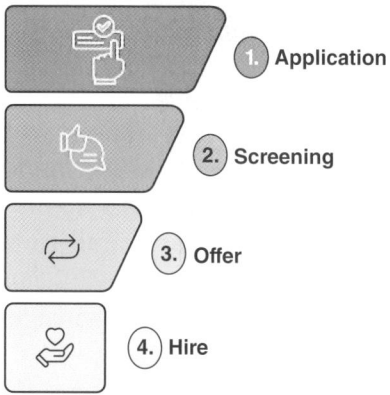

Figure 2.4 Side View of a Simplified Recruitment Funnel

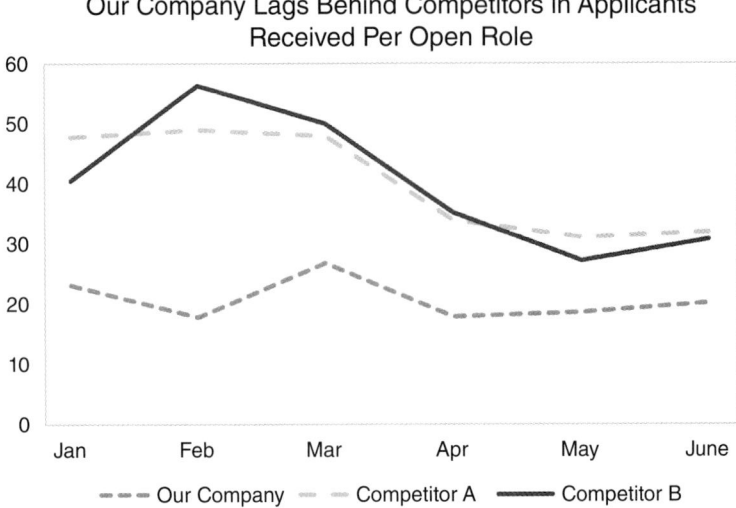

Figure 2.5　Applications per Role from January to June

ready by running some additional analysis beforehand to address these follow-up questions.

Finally, you looked to Glassdoor for some more data on the employer brand and interview process, which is displayed in Figure 2.6.

It is clear that our company interview experience is worse than competitor A, as our candidates report less positive experience and much more negative experience. In fact, we lag by about 50% in the candidates who say they have a positive experience during the interview.

As you dive into the specific comments, you've discovered several issues where candidates mention having too many rounds of interviews. There were also complaints about unprepared hiring managers and interviewers who appeared to have no knowledge about the role at all.

Now you are armed with preliminary insights to start thinking about putting together recommendations.

As you put together a presentation for your stakeholders, let's think about the headline and then the subheadline for this analysis

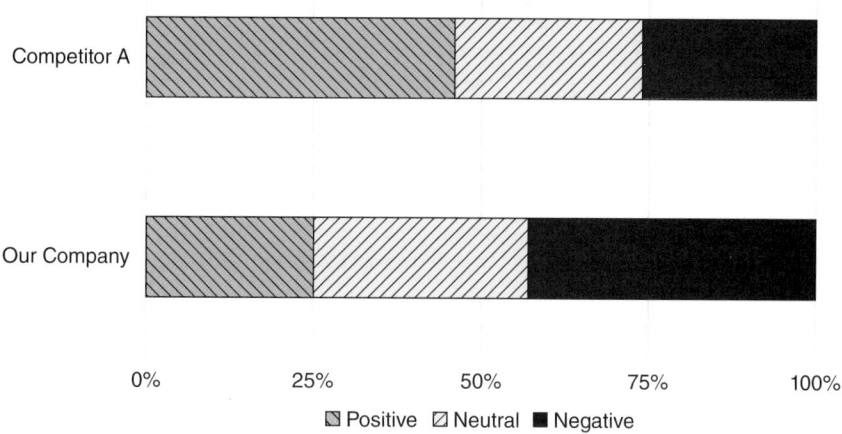

Figure 2.6 Glassdoor Interview Experience Comparisons

overall: "We get fewer candidates than our competitors and our lengthy recruiting process. Bad Glassdoor reviews hold us back."

That is not exactly catchy; let's try again.

Title: Why Can't We Attract Talent?
Subtitle: Data Reveals Hiring Process and Reputation Issues

Better, but there is not a sense of urgency. Let's try one more time.

Title: Time to Revamp: Company's Hiring Process Needs an Urgent Makeover
Subtitle: Data Shows 50% Interview Experience Gap, Glassdoor Reviews Need Attention

A note on step 3: I am not suggesting you create a story first and then find only data that support the claim. This is the slippery slope of data storytelling. Early in my career, I encountered managers and clients who requested that I create data visualization to support a position or opinion. It was very difficult to say no as a young analyst, but I knew my reputation was worth more than the temporary discomfort. It took courage and confidence for me to present all the data, including those that contradicted their opinions. It wasn't easy, but it was necessary. I know you may also encounter pressure at some point in your career, and I share from experience that my stakeholders respected me even more for saying no.

From Data to Insights: Visualization Dos and Don'ts

Close your eyes. Think of the worst data visualization you've seen recently. What made it so bad?

Is it the busyness of the chart?
Is it missing labels or legends to clearly explain the data points?
Is it the wrong choice of chart type for the data?

It's easier to point out what's wrong with someone else's chart than to create a great chart ourselves. Here are some dos and don'ts from my experience:

Do:

- Clearly label data points and have consistency within the chart. For example, keep the number format at one decimal point throughout.
- Have consistent axis values if you have multiples charts presented side-by-side.
- Select the right chart type for the data (line for trends, stacked bars for proportions, etc.)

Don't:

- Use more than five colors. It's tough to keep track of, even with legends. Keep to two to three colors if possible.
- Use 3D charts. It's very difficult to read and the third dimension doesn't add any value or information.
- Change the scale or proportion to fit a tight space. I've been there too. I know how tempting it is, but it impacts the quality of your visualization.

A Short Lesson About Colors

The best advice I received when I first started designing data charts is this: "Design in grayscale, add color after." The harsh truth I had to learn was, "If you can't tell your data story in grayscale, colors won't help you."

I like to use color to emphasize a point in the data story. For example, Figure 2.7 shows cigarette use by race and ethnicity data.

You can highlight a particular group to draw the audience's attention by using a different color, for example, the group with the highest usage on average (Figure 2.8).

Alternatively, you may want to highlight the usage of those who are White as a comparison point, as done in Figure 2.9. See how your eyes are instantly drawn to the darkest column on the chart.

Remember to start with gray and then add one additional color at a time. The color must serve a purpose.

Colors in your chart should be not only functional but also pleasing to the eye.

If you work with a big organization, the branding or marketing department has probably already created a document called

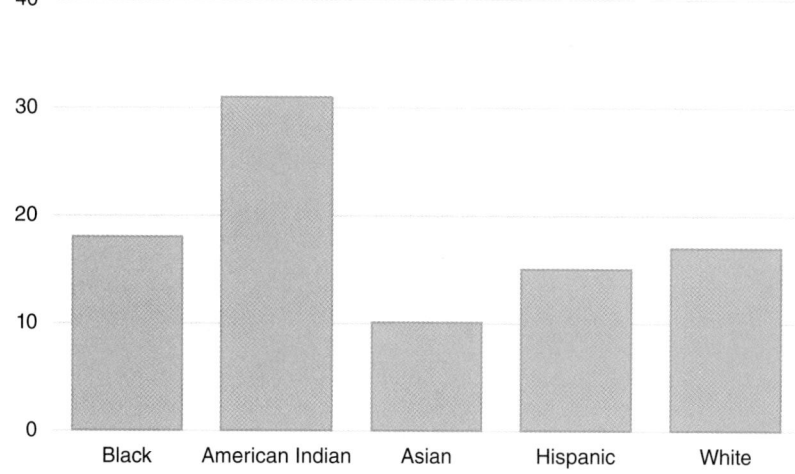

Figure 2.7 Cigarette Usage by Race/Ethnicity (percentage)

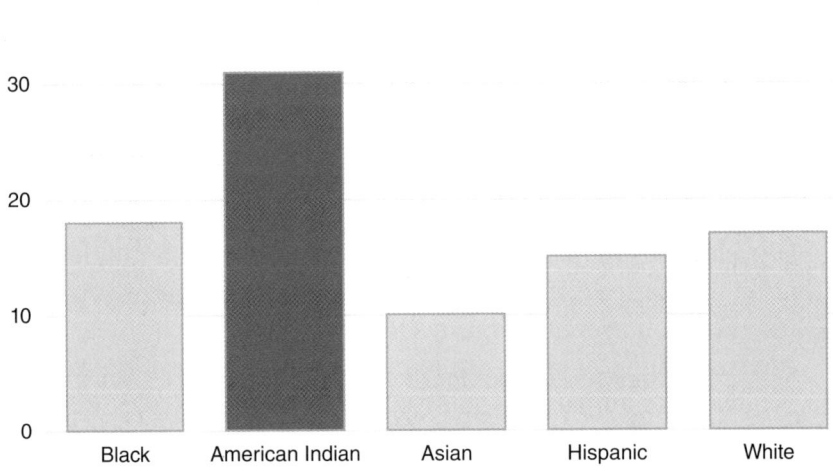

Figure 2.8   Cigarette Usage by Race/Ethnicity (percentage)

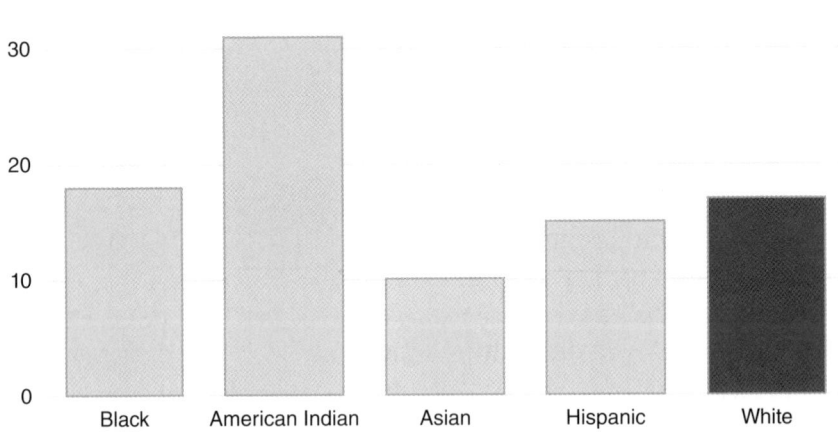

Figure 2.9   Cigarette Usage by Race/Ethnicity (percentage)

"company style guide" or "brand identity." Over the years, I've studied the style guide at various organizations. You may be required or recommended to use these colors for consistency.

Nonetheless, you'll want to determine which colors you'll use when there are multiple lines or bars on the graph. My team typically operates from a jointly created styles guide for dashboards and visualizations, which ensures our stakeholders see the same look and feel regardless of who created the data story.

Specifically, you can define multiple options for one-, two-, or three-colored charts and more.

If you want to see a comprehensive style guide, you can look up the one on the Tax Policy Center of Urban Institute's website.[2] Their guide clearly shows options for groups that are categorical versus sequential.

You can create a similar guide and determine the maximum number of colors you'll have in your charts. A general suggestion is to keep it under 10, and 5 if possible. You can always create a group called "other" by combing the smallest groups in your chart so you can keep the audience's attention on the most important takeaways.

Other books are available if you wish to dive deeper into colors and data visualization: *ColorWise: A Data Storyteller's Guide to the Intentional Use of Color* by Kate Strachnyi and *Visualize This: The FlowingData Guide to Design, Visualization, and Statistics* by Nathan Yau.

Dashboard Design Lessons

How should you design a dashboard with storytelling in mind? At one point or another in our lives, we've encountered a poorly designed dashboard where the data was not clear and the story was nonexistent. It's not difficult to know what not to do in creating a dashboard, but how do you create a compelling one for your stakeholders?

A simple process like the following has helped me when I led data visualization teams:

1. Align on the purpose of the dashboard with stakeholders.
2. Select the right KPIs to include.

3. Display the data clearly.
4. Finalize the layout for focus.
5. Add narratives for storytelling.

Aligning on Purpose

Before diving into data visualization, it's crucial to establish a clear purpose for your dashboard. Engage with stakeholders to understand their needs and objectives. What specific questions are they seeking answers to? What decisions do they need to make based on the data? By defining the purpose upfront, you ensure that the dashboard is tailored to their needs and ultimately delivers the desired impact.

Selecting the Right KPIs

KPIs are the building blocks of your story. They represent the critical metrics that drive your narrative and recommendations. Carefully select KPIs that are relevant to the dashboard's purpose and aligned with stakeholder objectives. Avoid overwhelming the user with too many metrics; focus on a concise set that effectively communicates the key insights. Be sure to align on the definition of these KPIs with your stakeholders as well.

Displaying Data Clearly

Once you've selected your KPIs, it's time to choose the right visualizations to present them. The visual language you use should be clear, concise, and easily interpretable. Consider using the following:

- **Bar charts:** Ideal for comparing discrete categories
- **Line charts:** Effective for showing trends over time
- **Scatter plots:** Useful for exploring relationships between two variables
- **Maps:** For visualizing geographic data
- **Gauges:** For highlighting progress toward targets

Finalizing the Layout for Focus

The layout of the dashboard is crucial for guiding the reader's eye and attention. Use visual hierarchy to draw attention to the most important information. Consider the following:

- **Spacing:** Provide ample white space to avoid clutter and improve readability.
- **Color:** Use color strategically to differentiate data points and highlight key areas. Make sure it's accessible and colorblind-friendly.
- **Font size and style:** Use font size and style to emphasize key elements and create visual interest. I suggest keeping it to only three different font sizes and use the same style if possible.
- **Grouping:** Group related metrics together to enhance coherence and understanding.

Adding Narratives for Storytelling

Data visualization is only part of the story. To bring the story to life, you need to weave a narrative around the data. Consider adding the following:

- **Titles and headings:** Use clear and concise titles and headings to provide context and guide the reader's understanding. My favorite tip is to use questions as titles where the data in the chart provide answers to the questions.
- **Callouts:** Use callouts to draw attention to key insights and emphasize actionable takeaways. This can be a hover-over text-box on an interactive dashboard, so it is not overcrowding the chart.
- **Interactive elements:** Incorporate interactive elements to enable exploratory analysis, such as drill-down capabilities or filters to slice and dice. You can also have correlation plots where users can update the axis.

Designing a dashboard for storytelling is an iterative process. It requires a deep understanding of your data, your audience, and the narrative you wish to convey. I often set up a series of update meetings with the stakeholders so they can provide input along the way.

It's also helpful to have testers who are not as familiar with the data so you can get honest feedback on whether the data story is clear and engaging.

How to Structure a Data Story

Let's talk about the structure of a data story. A story typically follows this structure:

Context
Conflict
Resolution

You can use this structure to draft your narrative. In the world of data storytelling, context is the problem statement. Conflict is the headline worthy data point and insight you've found. Resolution is the recommendation you're putting forward.

Let's walk through an example.
The problem:

We have engineering roles open in the city of LaLaLand and only 20% of the applicants are women. We know that locally the percentage of college grads in STEM is 45%. This disparity not only limits our access to a diverse range of talent but also hinders our ability to create a truly inclusive and innovative workplace.

The **context** is attracting female talent to engineering roles in LaLaLand.

The **conflict** in this problem is the low percentage of women applying for engineering roles relative to STEM graduates.

What would potential **resolution** look like?

We could recommend increasing the effort in attracting women to apply, which could include new recruiting initiatives or partnering with women in STEM nonprofits locally. It can also include additional research and fact-finding, such as checking Glassdoor reviews for interview process issues.

This is also an area where generative AI (GenAI) can help as well. You could ask GenAI to analyze the quality of your data story, without exposing confidential or sensitive information, of course. You could also ask GenAI to provide recommendations to make the story more compelling. As an example, I asked Gemini 1.5 for some assistance on making the story better, and it provided the following:

> LaLaLand boasts a vibrant STEM community, with 45% of college graduates in the field. However, our engineering roles in the city are attracting a significantly lower percentage of women applicants, currently only at 20%. This disparity not only limits our access to a diverse range of talent but also hinders our ability to create a truly inclusive and innovative workplace. We are committed to achieving a more representative engineering team that reflects the local market.
>
> To achieve this goal, we need to significantly increase the number of women applying to our engineering roles. Here are some concrete steps we can take:
>
> - **Boost Recruitment Efforts:** We could recommend increasing our efforts in attracting women to apply, which could include new recruiting initiatives, partnering with women in STEM non-profits locally, and actively promoting our company at women-focused career events.
> - **Analyze Interview Process:** We should conduct thorough research and fact-finding to understand potential barriers in our current interview process. This could involve checking Glassdoor reviews for feedback from female candidates, conducting internal interviews with hiring managers, and reviewing our interview questions for potential bias.
> - **Highlight Company Culture:** We need to actively showcase our company culture and demonstrate our commitment to diversity and inclusion. This could involve featuring women engineers in our marketing materials, highlighting our employee resource groups, and sharing stories about our initiatives to support women in STEM.

By taking these concrete steps, we can create a more welcoming and inclusive environment that attracts and retains top female talent, ultimately achieving a more representative engineering team that reflects the vibrant STEM community in LaLaLand."

From Insights to Action: Recommendations and Influencing

Your team of analysts spent weeks cleaning the data and performing comprehensive analysis. They create beautiful visuals and make a data-informed recommendation in the presentation. Your stakeholders said, "Thanks, that's interesting," but chose to ignore the recommendation completely. Sound familiar?

Every analytics team lead I've talked to has had the same experience. They feel frustrated and disappointed. Often there's no explanation. In my experience, this can happen for a few reasons even if your data story is compelling.

- Your recommendations cannot be implemented.
- The stakeholders you need to influence are not convinced.
- The power dynamics are not taken care of.

The list goes on. Overall, it is because the analytics team isn't able to influence without authority. "Influencing without authority" is an absolutely essential skill for analytics professionals to master and is a skill I've hired for and developed on my team over the years. When you are making a recommendation that needs to be implemented by someone else—you are trying to influence while you don't have the authority to decide.

Trust is key to being able to influence without authority. Without trust, your insights and recommendations fall on deaf ears and you won't be able to drive lasting change. How do you build trust with the key stakeholders? It's a question that has puzzled many data analytics teams. In his book, *The Speed of Trust* (2006), Stephen R. Covey provides a framework for building trust, which I'll outline in this context.

Covey's Trust Matrix is built around four cores of trust:

- Integrity
- Intent
- Capabilities
- Results

These cores are interconnected and interdependent, and each one is essential to building trust with the stakeholders.

Let's start with **Integrity**. Do your stakeholders believe you are transparent and honest in our interactions with them? When we're transparent about our data and methods, and we disclose limitations and caveats, we demonstrate integrity. We also show integrity when we admit when we don't know something.

Next is **Intent**. Do your stakeholders believe you have their best interests at heart? When we take the time to understand their needs, actively listen, show empathy and compassion, and put their interests first, we demonstrate intent. We're not just trying to push our own agenda or sell them on our latest and greatest idea. We're genuinely interested in solving their problem and helping them succeed.

Capabilities are also critical. This is the obvious one for most teams. Do your stakeholders believe we have the skills and expertise to deliver high-quality insights and recommendations? When we stay up-to-date with industry trends and best practices, develop business acumen, and communicate complex concepts effectively, we demonstrate capabilities. We show that we are knowledgeable and competent.

Finally, there's **Results**. Do your stakeholders believe you can deliver? When we set clear expectations and follow through on our commitments, we show that we can deliver. Additionally, if we also continuously improve and refine our insights and recommendations, we are demonstrating results.

By focusing on these four cores of trust, you can establish a strong foundation of trust with any stakeholder in the organization. Remember, trust is not a one-time event, but rather a continuous process that requires ongoing effort and conversations.

Change Management Pitfalls to Avoid

Following are some of the biggest pitfalls I ran into early in my career:

- Not knowing who the real decision-makers were
- Only hearing from my champions and not knowing who my resistors were
- Thinking that hearing something one time is enough to change someone's mind

Not Knowing Who the Real Decision-makers Were

Many of us are taught that the more senior someone is, the more power they have, so as long as the most senior leader signs off on an initiative, everything else will fall into place.

Not so fast.

In large and matrixed organizations, decision-making is not at all straight forward. There can be influential individuals who do not have an obvious title. I recall a seemingly simple ask of changing the employee survey vendor where my team had the expertise and was in charge of running the proposal—I understood incorrectly that having expertise means having the decision-making power. We were expected to provide expertise and recommendations and seek buy-in from other stakeholders across the organization to come to a final decision. It started with a couple of HR executives and turned into an entire steering committee with cross functional representation. Business-to-business (B2B) sales professionals know how hard this is to figure out from the outside. It is sometimes equally difficult to figure out while you are on the inside.

After that lesson, I heavily prioritized relationship building when I arrived in a new organization, especially those outside my own department, so I can have a more holistic approach. The perspectives from leaders outside my department became helpful when I had to approach an issue with enterprise-wide impact. They help me see outside my lane and in more than one occasion some of them ended up being the decision makers for my project.

Only Hearing from My Champions and Not Knowing Who My Resistors Were

It is absolutely critical you map out the champions and resistors as you approach any project that will result in change in how people experience work. I am being intentionally broad because I learned the hard way that even a small change could have a big impact on individuals in the organization I hadn't considered.

When I proposed to move a company's employee survey strategy from one long survey once a year to shorter surveys multiple times a year, I had overwhelmingly strong support from every C-suite leader. I thought it was going to be a piece of cake to roll out the change, and I couldn't have been more wrong.

I got a "Can we talk?" ping from an HR leader saying there were noises in the organization, and I needed a heads-up. I called them back immediately and could not believe what I heard. While the chief human resources officer (CHRO) was supportive of the change in strategy, the DEI team was very unhappy with the fact that a shorter survey meant fewer questions on DEI. They eventually shared their frustration with the CHRO and others within the HR function. I had to do some serious damage control at that point with the DEI team, and it was the result of my not understanding the impact. When I got on that call, I practiced active listening and was able to understand they were concerned the shortened survey conveyed the community DEI did not matter as much as before. I explained the new strategy would include both shortened regular surveys and the addition of a theme-specific pulse survey, and DEI would be one of those themes. "This new strategy shows we care about DEI more, not less than before," I said. It took some time to re build the trust between the DEI team and me, and it was a memorable lesson learned for me.

*Thinking Hearing Something One Time Is Enough to
Change Someone's Mind*

It's not.

There is neuroscience research that repetition helps, so if you think a presentation that is well-received is enough to change the stakeholders' minds, think again.

Do you know why companies drop a lot of money on ad campaigns that repeatedly show the same product or service to you? They want to make sure you don't just see their ad once, twice, or three times. They know that seeing something once won't change your mind, and it takes repeated attempts for a new behavior, such as buying their product, to emerge.

You'll be unable to run ads to get senior leaders on board in an organization. However, you can be prepared to have multiple conversations about the recommendations you are making to ensure success.

Change Management for Data Driven Decision-making

One of the change management frameworks I learned early on is the Change Acceleration Process (CAP) model. It has a total of seven steps:

1. **Leading change:** Leadership of the organization needs to consistently show a strong commitment to supporting change. There is a significant risk of failure if the organization lacks strong leadership commitment to the change initiatives.
2. **Creating a shared need:** People must see the need for change for it to be accepted and worked on. Reasons must be compelling and resonate not just for the leadership team but for everyone in the organization.
3. **Shaping a vision:** Leadership must present a clear vision of the impact on the organization after a successful change. The desired outcome should be clearly understood, have genuine reasons, and be widely accepted.

4. **Mobilizing commitment:** Once the first three steps are in place, momentum needs to be built toward the need for change. It should include engaging, identifying, planning, and analyzing the necessary changes.

5. **Making change last:** The challenge here is how to *maintain the gain.* This step is about learning from previous mistakes, adjusting the initiative if needed, and transforming the change into *how we do things here.* All of this will help make the change more permanent and sustain success.

6. **Monitoring progress:** Measuring how the change initiative is progressing, and celebrating when appropriate, will help to cement the change in the organization. Set benchmarks for success, and measure them often and objectively.

7. **Changing systems and structures:** To make the change permanent, the infrastructure must be set up to support it. If your current infrastructure (IT systems, HR policies, organizational design, etc.) is set up to support the previous state of the organization, they must be updated to support the future vision or the organization will not be able to make the change last.

Application

One of the most difficult shifts in organizations without a mature data-driven talent decision-making process is changing the promotion process. How would you use the seven-step CAP model to influence this change?

1. **Leading Change:** Build trust by showing how data have improved promotion decisions elsewhere. Frame data as a complement rather than replacement for intuition, helping them make better decisions. Involve them in the data analysis and interpretation so they can see the value firsthand.

2. **Creating a Shared Need:** Acknowledge their years of experience, but also point out the limitations of relying solely on intuition. Show how data can solve specific problems, like identifying high-potential individuals who might be overlooked.

Address their fear of change by emphasizing that data is a tool to support their decision-making, not replace it.

3. **Shaping a Vision:** Start small with a pilot program in a specific department or role. Be transparent about the data used, the methodology, and the decision-making process. Highlight early successes to demonstrate the positive impact of data-driven promotions.

4. **Mobilizing Commitment:** Find individuals within the leadership team who are open to data-driven approaches. Involve HR and talent management professionals to collect, analyze, and present data effectively. Foster a culture where insights are valued and shared.

5. **Making Change Last:** Continuously track the impact of data-driven promotions and share results with leaders. Be prepared to adapt the approach based on feedback and evolving needs. Celebrate successes to solidify the value of data-driven decision-making.

6. **Monitoring Progress**: Establish KPIs to measure the effectiveness of data-driven promotions, such as time-to-hire, candidate quality, employee retention, and diversity metrics. Track progress against these metrics and communicate results to stakeholders.

7. **Changing Systems and Structures**: Update HR processes and systems to support data-driven decision-making in the promotion process. Implement new HR policies and create new roles or train individuals to support data analysis.

By applying CAP's principles in a conversational way, you can gradually shift the mindset of senior leaders, demonstrating the value of data and fostering a culture of data-driven decision-making in hiring and promotions.

Three Biggest Myths Around Storytelling

There are many obstacles that hold people back from using storytelling effectively in a professional setting. The most common myths around storytelling I have heard are the following:

"The data speaks for itself." No, it doesn't, unfortunately. This myth is a particularly dangerous one because we have all heard it before. While data can be powerful, it's unlikely self-explanatory by itself. Can an Excel spreadsheet with hundreds of rows and columns of numbers "speak for itself"? Because data are usually multidimensional, analysis of the data is first required to extract the insights and display them in a digestible format. Data can also be misinterpreted without appropriate context, making the storyteller's job a critical one. Overall, you need the other elements of a data story, visuals, and narrative, to make a data story self-explanatory.

"A good chart is all I need." Data visualization is not the entire story, only part of it. Even the most visually appealing chart without explanation will lack meaning to truly engage the audience. As mentioned in the examples earlier, charts should support a narrative rather than replace it. Also, a good chart for one audience may be unclear and confusing for another. We know that technical and business audiences have different preferences when it comes to data visualization.

"You always need to tell stories with data." There are times when the data are so straightforward that it answers a yes or no question without needing a story to do it. For example: "Is the employee attrition rate higher this year than last year?" If the data show a clear increase, you don't need a complex story. However, you can anticipate questions from someone reading this data immediately, such as "Why is the attrition rate higher?" and "Which particular group should we pay more attention to?" Providing a brief explanation of the why based on simple analysis would be helpful.

GenAI as Copilot in Data Analysis and Storytelling

In the era of GenAI, it can seem like it is a solution to every problem—like you suddenly have a hammer, and every problem is now a nail.

Can you leverage GenAI to do the storytelling for you? Not quite 100%. Here's where and when it is very helpful.

In an *MIT Sloan Management Review* column, Ganes Kesari proposes a 2x2 matrix based on the *data insight approach* and the *level of information that users need* to determine whether GenAI would be a value add.[3] When the level of information users need is lower, Kesari recommends GenAI tool for both exploratory and explanatory work. On the other hand, when the information users need is sophisticated or dynamic, such as what-if questions, then a GenAI tool is less effective than an interactive dashboard. If the question is explanatory in nature and the level of information users need is sophisticated, this would require a comprehensive data story that AI can't easily handle automatically or conversationally. That doesn't mean you can't leverage GenAI to create part of the data story; it simply means that you can't deploy a chatbot for this level of questions.

Using GenAI for less complex data storytelling needs could save lots of effort and speed up insight delivery. This could also help organizations focus human effort and attention on the more specialized use cases of complex data stories, where expert care and the human touch are needed to empower decision makers.

Kesari states in his column:

> Today, AI has the ability to understand the business context and discover hidden data insights. These insights can then be presented conversationally via interactive chat to help the user absorb and act. For example, business intelligence (BI) tools such as Power BI or Tableau can be infused with generative AI capabilities to explain insights and interpret takeaways. Early generative AI integrations exist already, such as Copilot for Power BI[4] and Einstein Copilot for Tableau AI[5]. Even better, these insights could be surfaced through conversational interfaces rather than waiting for users to open dashboards and consume them visually. Hence, this is another area ready for disruption by AI chat interfaces.

In September 2021, Gartner predicted that data stories will be the most widespread way of consuming analytics by 2025, and that augmented analytics techniques will generate 75% of these stories automatically.[6]

My own experience with Microsoft Copilot has shown me that a lot of the basic training efforts analytics teams or learning teams have traditionally delivered may no longer be needed. If the user can have conversations with a dashboard in plain language, rather than having to figure out how to slice and dice the data to answer their questions, the adoption may be much higher.

Now that we know where GenAI can help, let's talk about the specifics. After giving hands-on GenAI workshops to data teams, I've turned these lessons into frameworks that are easy to remember and practical to use.

Winning Frameworks for Prompt Engineering

Following are frameworks that you can apply when you want to use GenAI for storytelling. I'd encourage you to try all of these frameworks and see what responses you receive.

Data Analysis and Storytelling

1. R-T (Role-Task):
   Description: RT prompts help clarify the role and task the AI system needs to provide.
   - Example: "Act as a data analytics expert and run a trend analysis of the average tenure of engineering directors in the last 5 years."
   - Example: "Act as a visualization expert and create an interactive dashboard from these data."
2. T-A-G (Task-Action-Goal):
   Description: TAG prompts define a specific task, action and a clear goal to accomplish.

- Example: "Analyze these survey comments, identify key themes and sentiment, with the goal to provide a summary of recommendations on employee safety."

3. R-I-S-E (Role-Input-Steps-Expectations):
Description: RISE prompts start with the role, similar to RT prompts, and then list out specific input and describe the steps to be taken for meeting certain expectations.

- Example: "Act as an analytics expert and use these data to create a short summary using these steps, first highlighting year-over-year trends, then identify outliers, and finally recommend follow-up analysis. The summary is going to be precise, clear, and data-informed for the CEO to make a decision on the next steps for the regional business."

4. S-P-I-C-E (Situation-Problem-Impact-Context-Emotion):
Description: SPICE prompts are great for storytelling when you are running short on ideas and need help getting started. It includes the elements needed for a story.

- Example: "Write a story about an employee who faced a problem with our onboarding process due to unclear instructions, which impacted their employee experience as a new hire and made them frustrated."
(Situation: new hire onboarding
Problem: unclear instructions during onboarding
Impact: negative employee experience
Context: employee feedback
Emotion: Frustration)

Advanced Analytics and GenAI

GenAI can help with advanced analytics in several ways.

It is best to be specific rather than using a "see what we can find" approach. While GenAI can understand plain language like "provide a summary of findings from this dataset," it does better with specific analytics requests. For example, "Can you calculate the correlation coefficient between 'age' and 'education completed' in the attached dataset and test its statistical significance?" and "Can you identify clusters of individuals with similar income?" work well from my experience.

Notice that you still need to have some foundational knowledge of statistical analysis to be able to know whether the suggested approach is valid.

For instance, the second prompt, "Can you identify clusters of individuals with similar income?" resulted in the Python codes shown in Figure 2.10. While there are explanations for the individual steps, this would be difficult to understand for someone who hasn't seen or used Python before. More importantly, you'd need to know whether K-means is the correct method for this ask. Finally, if you had copied and pasted the codes into Python and run into issues, it might be very challenging to debug because you haven't used the language before. The additional difficulty is that GenAI output looks so convincing—it almost makes us wonder, "How could it be wrong?"

Automation and Collaboration with AI

One of the areas where we have seen lots of AI adoption is in automation of manual and repetitive tasks. When it comes to reporting, the scheduling function from any system was celebrated and loved. However, most systems do not offer the out-of-box look that organizations prefer, so traditionally a team of analysts spent hours formatting a report that is ready for consumption.

Now you can ask your favorite GenAI tool this question: "Can you help me automate an email with weekly sales report data to my manager, at 8 a.m. on Mondays?"

You'll likely receive suggestions and how you'd do this automation with different tools.

So, you can be more specific and ask, "What if I want to email a summary of sales by region and weekly trends to my manager every Monday at 8 a.m. CT? Assume I have Microsoft Power Automate and I can't use Python very well."

```python
import pandas as pd
from sklearn.preprocessing import LabelEncoder
from sklearn.cluster import KMeans
import matplotlib.pyplot as plt
import seaborn as sns

# Load the dataset
file_path = 'Sample_HealthAsianData.csv'
data = pd.read_csv(file_path)

# Drop rows with missing values in the 'Income' column
income_data = data[['Income']].dropna()

# Encode income categories into numerical values
label_encoder = LabelEncoder()
income_data['Income'] = label_encoder.fit_transform(income_data['Income'])

# Determine the optimal number of clusters using the elbow method
wcss = []  # within-cluster sum of squares
for i in range(1, 11):
    kmeans = KMeans(n_clusters=i, random_state=42)
    kmeans.fit(income_data)
    wcss.append(kmeans.inertia_)

# Plot the elbow method graph
plt.plot(range(1, 11), wcss)
plt.title('Elbow Method')
plt.xlabel('Number of clusters')
plt.ylabel('WCSS')
plt.show()

# Apply KMeans with the optimal number of clusters (e.g., 3 clusters)
kmeans = KMeans(n_clusters=3, random_state=42)
income_data['Cluster'] = kmeans.fit_predict(income_data)

# Add the cluster labels back to the original dataset
data['Income Cluster'] = pd.merge(data, income_data, left_index=True, right_index=True)['Clus
ter']

# Display the number of individuals in each cluster
print(data['Income Cluster'].value_counts())

# Display some sample data from each cluster
for cluster in range(3):
    print(f"\nCluster {cluster}:")
    print(data[data['Income Cluster'] == cluster].head())

# Plot the clusters
plt.figure(figsize=(10, 6))
sns.scatterplot(x='Age', y='Education Completed', hue='Income Cluster', data=data, palette='v
iridis')
plt.title('Clusters of Individuals by Income')
plt.xlabel('Age')
plt.ylabel('Education Completed')
plt.legend(title='Income Cluster')
plt.show()
```

Figure 2.10   GenAI Response Illustrating Python Codes to the Prompt "Can You Identify Clusters of Individuals with Similar Income?"

Llama, or Large Language Model Meta AI, is a family of large language models (LLMs) released by Meta AI. The version Llama 3 70B provided the detailed response to my previous prompt in the following box:

With Microsoft Power Automate (formerly Microsoft Flow), you can create a workflow to automate the process of sending a sales summary report to your manager every Monday at 8 a.m. CT. Since you're not familiar with Python, we'll focus on using Power Automate's visual interface to design the workflow.

Prerequisites:

- You have a Microsoft Power Automate account.
- You have a data source containing sales data, such as a SharePoint list, Excel file, or a CRM system (e.g., Dynamics, Salesforce).
- You have the necessary permissions to access the data source and send emails.

Step-by-Step Guide:

Step 1: Create a new flow.
1. Log in to your Microsoft Power Automate account and click on "Create from blank" to start a new flow.
2. Give your flow a name, such as "Weekly Sales Report to Manager."

Step 2: Add a trigger.
- Click on the "Add an action" button and search for "Recurrence".
- Select the "Recurrence" trigger and set the following settings:
  - Frequency: Weekly
  - At: 8:00 AM
  - Time zone: Central Time (US & Canada)
  - On: Monday
- Click "Add" to save the trigger.

(continued)

(continued)

Step 3: Connect to your data source.
- Click on the "Add an action" button and search for the connector related to your data source (e.g., SharePoint, Excel, Dynamics, Salesforce).
- Select the connector and authenticate with your data source if prompted.
- Configure the action to retrieve the sales data you need for the report. For example:
  - If using SharePoint, select the list and specify the columns you want to retrieve (e.g., Region, Sales Amount, Date).
  - If using Excel, select the file and specify the range of cells containing the sales data.

Step 4: Group and summarize data by region.
- Click on the "Add an action" button and search for "Group by."
- Select the "Group by" action and configure it to group the sales data by region.
- Click on the "Add an action" button again and search for "Sum."
- Select the "Sum" action and configure it to calculate the total sales amount for each region.

Step 5: Calculate weekly trends.
- Click on the "Add an action" button and search for "Filter array."
- Select the "Filter array" action and configure it to filter the sales data by date, selecting only the records from the current week.
- Click on the "Add an action" button again and search for "Sum."
- Select the "Sum" action and configure it to calculate the total sales amount for the current week.

Step 6: Create a summary email.
- Click on the "Add an action" button and search for "Send an email."
- Select the "Send an email" action and configure it to send an email to your manager's email address.

- In the email body, use the "Dynamic content" feature to add the following information:
  - A table or list displaying the sales summary by region (use the "Group by" and "Sum" actions from Step 4).
  - A section highlighting the weekly trends (use the "Filter array" and "Sum" actions from Step 5).

Step 7: Save and test the flow.

- Click "Save" to save the flow.
- Test the flow by clicking the "Test" button to ensure it runs successfully and sends the email to your manager.

Tips and Variations:

- Use Power Automate's conditional logic to handle errors or missing data.
- Consider adding additional details to the email, such as top-performing regions or salespeople.
- If you have multiple data sources, you can use Power Automate's "Join" action to combine the data before summarizing and sending the report.
- To make the report more interactive, consider using Power Automate's "Create a file" action to generate a PDF or Excel file and attach it to the email.

By following these steps, you'll have a Power Automate flow that sends a weekly sales summary report to your manager every Monday at 8 a.m. CT.

Another way to start collaborating with AI for organizations with Microsoft products is to leverage Copilot. You can use it within Excel for common tasks such as identifying trends and patterns, creating charts, and generating pivot tables.

Example Prompts:

- "Analyze the attrition rates over the past three years and identify any significant trends or patterns."

- "Create a line chart showing the trend in employee engagement index over the last 12 months."
- "Create a pivot table to analyze the distribution of employee tenure across different departments."

In this chapter, we discussed the three Cs of successful data storytelling along with when and how you can leverage GenAI for storytelling. We also cover design principles for dashboard creations, since dashboards are one of the main mechanisms for delivering insights. We ended with prompting frameworks and tips for using GenAI for storytelling and advanced analytics. With GenAI at our fingertips, there has never been a better time to tell compelling stories with data in the workplace. What framework will you leverage from this chapter to tell your data story next?

Notes

1. Dykes, B. (2022). *Contextualized insights: Six ways to put your numbers in context* [online]. Available at: https://www.effectivedatastorytelling.com/post/contextualized-insights-six-ways-to-put-your-numbers-in-context

2. Tax Policy Center. (2014). *Tax Policy Center data visualization style guide* [online]. Available at: https://apps.urban.org/tpc-styleguide/public.html

3. Kesari, G. (2024). The enduring power of data storytelling in the generative AI era [online]. *MIT Sloan Management Review*. Available at: https://sloanreview.mit.edu/article/the-enduring-power-of-data-storytelling-in-the-generative-ai-era/

4. Manis, K. (2023). *Empower power BI users with Microsoft Fabric and Copilot*. Microsoft Power BI Blog [online]. Available at: https://powerbi.microsoft.com/en-us/blog/empower-power-bi-users-with-microsoft-fabric-and-copilot/

5. Nichols, N. and Wang, H. (n.d.). *What is Tableau AI?* [online]. Tableau. Available at: https://www.tableau.com/blog/what-is-tableau-ai

6. Wiles, J. (2021). *Data & analytics trends CFOs can't ignore* [online]. Gartner. Available at: https://www.gartner.com/en/articles/4-data-analytics-trends-cfos-can-t-afford-to-ignore

Chapter 3

The Intersection of DEI and Well-being

Rachel, a classmate of mine in International Finance, was celebrating her 20th birthday when our professor asked the class about their weekend plans. We were all graduating seniors, and Rachel was younger by a couple of years. As we discussed our plans, the professor casually inquired, "Oh, what number are you celebrating?"

The question seemed harmless, but Rachel's eyes widened, and she stammered, "I'm finally turning 20." A ripple of laughter swept through the room, and the professor added fuel to the fire, "What did you say? You're turning 16 and finally old enough to get a driver's license?"

The laughter grew louder, and Rachel's face turned a deep shade of crimson. I felt a pang of sympathy for her, remembering the countless times I'd been teased for being younger than my peers. I didn't tell anyone I was actually the same age as Rachel. And I certainly wasn't about to now. I worried that I too would become a target of ridicule. The desire to belong was so strong that I often suppressed my voice, afraid of being excluded. Witnessing Rachel's pain, however, I realized that we were not alone in our experiences.

We have all felt excluded at one point or another in our life. Think about the last time you felt excluded. What made you feel that way? Did you share that feeling with anyone? Think about how well you felt at that point. Likely not very well.

There is a strong connection between feeling *included* at work and feeling *well*. In fact, employees expect a sense of belonging at work. Ninety-four percent of respondents reported that it's somewhat or very important to them that their workplace be somewhere they feel they belong, according to the American Psychological Association 2023 Work in America survey.[1] In this chapter, we will discuss in detail how organizations should pay attention to the interplay between DEI and employee well-being.

The Interplay of DEI and Mental Health

The intersection of DEI and mental health is a critical area that requires both attention and action from organizations. By understanding the unique challenges faced by diverse populations and implementing integrated, culturally competent strategies, employers can create a more inclusive and supportive work environment. This holistic approach not only enhances employee well-being but also drives business success.

What role does demographic background play in mental health? Reports from Columbia University suggest that a Black adult is 20% more likely than a White adult to experience a serious mental health concern.[2] The analysis from CARE International shows that 27% of women experienced increased mental health struggles due to COVID-19, compared with 10% of men.[3] Additional research found that people with low incomes are up to three times more likely to experience depression and anxiety.[4] Overall, BIPOC (Black, Indigenous, and people of color) individuals are at higher risk for experiencing mental health challenges.

Access to mental health care also varies. The data reported by the Substance Abuse and Mental Health Services Administration (SAMHSA) show that of the adults who accessed mental health services over one year, 16.6% were White, 15.6% were American Indian or Alaska Native, 8.6% were Black, 7.3% were Hispanic, and just 4.9% were Asian.[5]

The reasons for such low rates of access to care among BIPOC groups include lack of transportation or childcare, fear of racism and discrimination, different cultural perceptions about mental health, hesitation about taking time off work, and language barriers, to name just a few.

Additionally, employees who belong to these populations face many barriers to finding mental health providers who understand their culture, background, and identity. An overwhelming majority of mental health professionals are White, which can pose challenges for BIPOC individuals seeking culturally competent care. Increasing diversity within the mental health workforce is crucial to providing effective and empathetic support to all individuals. The American Psychological Association's Center for Workforce Studies reports the following demographic data:

- In 2015, 86% of psychologists in the US workforce were White, 5% were Asian, 5% were Hispanic, 4% were Black, and 1% were multiracial or from other racial/ethnic groups.
- The health service psychology workforce was 88% White and 12% BIPOC.
- The trends may be improving as a third (32%) of psychology doctorates earned in 2016 were awarded to BIPOC, and 68% were awarded to Whites.[6]

Identity Covering and Workplace Well-being

"Identity covering" is a significant issue whereby employees hide aspects of their identity to fit in. This practice can severely undermine workplace well-being and DEI efforts. It is certainly exhausting to have to hide part of who you are, including having to constantly watch what you say and how you dress in order to blend in and be more like the rest of the group at work.

Some examples of **covering** can range from parents with toddlers downplaying their need for flexibility to take their children to doctors' appointments to Chinese Americans avoiding mentioning Lunar New Year during the celebration. It is human to want to belong so when we feel unsafe to show part of us, we are naturally going to hide it.

Covering part or all of one's identity can impact an employee's well-being in significant ways. Research by Deloitte and New York University Professor of Law Kenji Yoshino reports 75% of employees cover in the workplace (up to 94% of diverse talent) and say that covering is "somewhat" to "extremely" detrimental to their sense of self.[7]

Employees who lack a sense of belonging may experience additional stress and burnout, leading to disconnection from their roles and colleagues. On the other hand, when employees feel a sense of belonging, they are more resilient during challenging times. This sense of support improves engagement and motivates them to collaborate and ask for help from their manager or colleagues when needed.

Mental Health Support at Work

A study in 2023 by the Hartford and the National Alliance on Mental Illness (NAMI) found Black US workers face greater barriers to mental health support in the workplace compared with other US workers.[8] Specifically, the study found that Black workers were more likely to rate their mental health as "fair/poor" and were less likely to say their company had empathetic leadership and an open, inclusive work environment that encourages a mental health dialogue. Also, Black American workers were more likely to say they encounter difficulty in discussing mental health in the workplace due to their race/ethnicity, cultural background, and gender identity. Moreover, Black workers were more likely than White workers to say they have experienced exclusion, hostility, a culture of inequity, microaggressions, and discrimination at their job that affected their mental health. White working Americans were more likely than Black and Latino workers to report a strong personal connection with coworkers, a sense of belonging at work, and alignment with company values.

Following are survey questions included in the study:

- I am/would be comfortable talking to my coworkers about my mental health.
- My company's leadership, including managers/supervisors, are empathetic and take a genuine interest in employees' lives.
- My company provides employees with flexibility in work schedules to get mental health help.

- My company has an open and inclusive work environment that encourages a dialogue about mental health.
- I feel comfortable being my true self at work.
- I have a sense of belonging at my work.
- My values align with my company's values.
- I have strong personal connections with my coworkers.

In my conversation with organizational psychologist, former mental health therapist, and author of *Yes, You Can Talk About Mental Health at Work (Here's Why and How to Do It Really Well)*, Melissa Doman has the following advice to organizations: "We have to look at mental health through the lens of individual experience. Yes, we all medically have mental health. That doesn't mean that we view or feel the same way about this topic that is so deeply personal and unique. Organizations will not understand the true complexities of mental health if they don't take personal influences into account around this subject."

From the research on well-being and DEI, two themes stand out:

- Well-being cannot be achieved without inclusion. Covering has a negative impact on employee well-being and engagement.
- Employers must be mindful of the mental healthcare access disparity between groups as it is well-documented that people of color face barriers to obtaining quality access.

The Role of Data and AI

Let's explore how you can leverage data and AI in your organization to better understand the issues of mental well-being and DEI.

Issue 1: Well-being cannot be achieved without inclusion. Covering has a negative impact on employee well-being and engagement.

A few ideas to get started. Do you know the extent to which the employees in your organization cover? "Uncovering culture" by Deloitte's DEI Institute™ and the Meltzer Center for Diversity, Inclusion, and Belonging at NYU School of Law finds a staggering 60% of employees, and up to 94% of diverse talent, engage in "covering" at work. The point isn't to find out whether more or less than 60% of employees in your organization engage in cover, but rather to discover the "why" and identify particular areas that need help.

Individuals cover because they don't feel safe showing themselves, so it'd be difficult to directly ask about whether someone is covering via a survey. There is also a phenomenon of "covering by proxy," meaning individuals can cover on behalf of someone else. For instance, a White employee with an adopted Asian child doesn't advocate for Asian employees within their organization.

Alternatively, you can use data analytics to uncover patterns that reveal potential biases and barriers to inclusion. Specifically, here are key ways to leverage data and AI.

Collaboration Data Can Tell the Hidden Story

Imagine being able to visualize the collaboration patterns within your organization. Who is working with whom? Who is being left out of projects? Who is having regulation conversations with their team members? This is where Organizational Network Analysis (ONA) comes in. By analyzing communication and work patterns, you can identify potential bottlenecks and areas where certain groups or individuals may be feeling excluded. You can also map out decision-making connections within the organization.[9]

If your data reveal that certain departments or individuals of certain characteristics are consistently left out of key meetings, it could be a sign of unconscious bias or a lack of intentional inclusivity. By recognizing these patterns, you can take proactive steps to address them, ensuring that everyone has a seat at the table.

The Power of Natural Language Processing

Implement anonymous surveys: Regular surveys can help you gauge the level of psychological safety and inclusion in your organization. Surveys are a great way to gather feedback from employees, but text can be time-consuming to analyze. By applying natural language processing (NLP) to comments from surveys, you can uncover hidden themes and sentiments that may not be immediately apparent.

For example, NLP might reveal that certain groups of employees are consistently expressing feelings of frustration or exclusion in their comments. This could be due to a lack of representation, inadequate resources, or a sense of being undervalued. By identifying these themes, you can develop targeted initiatives to address these concerns and create a more inclusive work environment.

Next you can run correlation analysis with any well-being-related data or the key performance indicator for well-being your organization uses. For example, you can correlate mindfulness program participation or well-being measures with demographic data and inclusion metrics. You can also correlate the well-being metrics with questions around psychological safety, belonging, or inclusion. Generative AI (GenAI) can help with the code for such analysis if you need additional guidance.

Listening Sessions for Human Touch

While data are valuable, it's equally important to listen to the human stories behind the numbers. Many leading organizations host regular listening sessions to ensure they are hearing from employees. These sessions provide a safe space for employees to share their experiences, suggestions, and concerns without fear of judgment.

By actively listening to employees and their lived experiences, you can gain a deeper understanding of the barriers that prevent them from feeling included and valued. This human-centered approach can provide added context to data collected via surveys or ONA and help you develop more appropriate solutions.

You can leverage AI meeting note-taking technology to capture and summarize the conversations to speed up the process, provided it does not violate privacy policies and regulations. Once the conversations are turned into text format, they can be combined with other data gathered above for a more comprehensive analysis.

By combining collaboration pattern analysis, NLP on surveys, and listening sessions, you can identify areas of exclusion, understand why employees are covering, and design initiatives to address these issues. One related topic that deserves a focused discussion is psychological safety.

Complexity of Psychological Safety

When it comes to measuring covering and barriers to psychological safety, it's important to note that psychological safety is not a black-and-white measure. There is a spectrum of four stages, as developed by social scientist and author of *The 4 Stages of Psychological Safety*, Timothy R. Clarke, where we feel

- included,
- safe to learn,
- safe to contribute, and
- safe to challenge the status quo.

Data and AI can help gauge the level of psychological safety in your organization in numerous ways.

Inclusion

At this stage, members feel safe to belong to the team. They are comfortable being present, do not feel excluded, and feel like they are appreciated.

- **Representation Analysis:** Use data to analyze the demographics and representation of employees across different levels and departments. Identify areas where underrepresentation exists and track progress over time.
- **Employee Surveys:** Leverage sentiment analysis to analyze employee feedback surveys, identifying areas where employees feel excluded. This can reveal specific issues related to inclusion, such as lack of opportunities for advancement.
- **Network Analysis:** Use data to map employee networks and identify potential silos or barriers to collaboration. This can help identify opportunities to foster cross-functional connections and promote a more inclusive environment.

Safe to Learn

At this stage, members can learn through asking questions. Team members here may be able to experiment, make small mistakes, and seek help.

- **Performance Reviews and 360 Surveys:** Use AI to analyze the feedback on performance reviews and 360 surveys to identify themes of proactive learning and learning from mistakes or risk-taking.
- **Knowledge Sharing:** One of the ways we learn is by sharing what we know. Identifying ways individuals are sharing their knowledge internally is an indication of proactive learning.
- **Engagement Surveys:** Include questions around risk-taking or experiment to measure on a regular basis and compare the response across different demographic groups for more insights.

Safe to Contribute

At this stage, members feel safe to contribute their own ideas, without fear of embarrassment or ridicule. This is a more challenging state, because volunteering your own ideas can increase the psychosocial vulnerability of team members.

- **Contribution Analysis:** Use AI-powered systems to analyze airtime of various demographic groups to ensure that all voices are heard and considered. Chats on project channels can also be analyzed in a similar way—do the ideas from historically marginalized groups get the same reactions as others?
- **Performance Reviews and 360 Surveys:** Use AI to analyze the feedback on performance reviews and 360 surveys to understand how feedback providers describe the individuals. Do certain groups of employees appear more "creative" or "innovate" than others?

   Given the research showing there is often bias in performance reviews, organizations must be both cautious and proactive in identifying gaps and potential issues. Around 76% of high-performing women receive negative feedback compared to only 2% of men, according to a new report from management software company Textio, which analyzed performance reviews for more than 23,000 workers across 250 organizations.[10]

   Kieran Snyder, cofounder of Textio, tells *Fortune* this has largely to do with managers' unconscious bias—women are judged more critically and on a more personal level than men.

- **Engagement Surveys:** Ask questions around sharing ideas in the engagement survey and identify potential areas for improvement. Running a correlation analysis can also help identify specific factors that contribute to employee engagement.

Safe to Challenge the Status Quo

At the highest level of safety, members can question others' ideas or suggest significant changes to ideas, plans, or existing ways of working.

- **Sentiment Analysis:** Use AI to analyze employee communication channels, including internal messaging platforms like slack and external social media channels, to understand the sentiment around change and challenging the status quo. Do employees feel frustrated by "this is how we have always done it"?
- **Engagement Surveys:** Ask questions around whether employees felt comfortable challenging someone senior to them on an idea in the engagement survey. Identify the difference between demographic groups.
- **Innovation and Experimentation:** The organization can create an idea-thon type event to give employees space to express new ideas and challenge existing assumptions. Are there groups of the organization where employees are more open to sharing?

Once you are able to understand in depth the level of psychological safety overall and any disparity between groups, you can create strategies to remove biases and barriers to inclusion.

Issue 2: Employers must be mindful of the mental healthcare access disparity between groups.

It's well documented that social-economic factors pose barriers to individuals seeking medical care, whether it's physical or mental healthcare.

These barriers to care, intricately woven into the fabric of society, can significantly impede access to appropriate healthcare and ultimately impact an individual's quality of life. Among these obstacles, the social determinants of health (SDOH) emerge as particularly potent forces, shaping both the individual's capacity to engage with healthcare systems and their overall health outcomes.

The SDOH encompass a broad range of social, economic, and environmental factors that influence health status:

- **Safe Transportation:** Limited access to reliable and affordable transportation can significantly hinder individuals from reaching healthcare facilities, especially in remote and rural areas or for those who cannot take off hours from work to seek care.
- **Discrimination:** Experiences of discrimination based on race, ethnicity, gender, sexual orientation, immigrant-status, or other social identities can lead to stress, anxiety, and mistrust of healthcare systems, ultimately deterring individuals from seeking care. There may be stories in the community from past experiences of family and friends that prevent them from trying to get care due to fear.
- **Income:** Low socioeconomic status often translates to limited access to quality healthcare, healthy food, safe housing, and educational opportunities, all of which directly impact health outcomes. The loss of income from taking a day or a few hours off may be a significant barrier to care.
- **Language and Literacy Skills:** Individuals with low literacy skills may struggle to navigate complex healthcare systems, understand medical information, or effectively communicate their needs to healthcare providers. Those who aren't native speakers may experience additional challenges in seeking and receiving care.

How about access to mental healthcare at work? Many organizations provide free or subsidized access via employee assistance programs (EAPs) and rarely do we hear about the disparity in the usage. There is no doubt the usage data is private and sensitive. However, it can be useful to understand the lived experiences of employees from marginalized racial and gender groups who are struggling with mental health issues but are hesitant to seek help, particularly through EAPs. Here are some questions to ponder:

- How can data be collected and analyzed to identify potential disparities in EAP access and utilization?
- What factors, such as lack of awareness, stigma, or systemic barriers, contribute to these disparities?
- How can organizations leverage data to develop targeted interventions and policies addressing EAP access disparities?
- How can leaders create a culture of openness and support for mental health, regardless of race or gender, and ensure that EAPs are effectively marketed and utilized by all employees?
- What role can EAP providers play in ensuring that their services are accessible and relevant to diverse employee populations?
- How can sharing personal stories help to break down stigma and raise awareness about these issues, particularly regarding EAP utilization?
- What are the challenges and opportunities associated with using storytelling to advocate for change in EAP access and accessibility?
- What are the ethical considerations involved in sharing personal stories about mental health struggles, particularly when focusing on EAP access?
- What innovative solutions and technologies could be implemented to create a more equitable and inclusive mental health system, particularly with regard to EAP access?

Given the sensitivity, it is helpful to obtain both quantitative and qualitative data on EAP usage or experience. I've helped benefits departments design surveys to understand the level of awareness and satisfaction with various benefits programs, but these often do not include specific questions around mental healthcare. If you want to have useful data to understand potential gaps in the experience among groups, interviews and focus groups may provide higher quality data with the context you need.

Why Should Leaders Care?

According to the article "The Overlooked Link Between Belonging & Workplace Well-being," employees are 71% less likely to experience burnout and are 69% less likely to actively look for a new job when they feel that their employer is concerned about their mental and emotional health. There is a link between feeling like an employer cares and an employee's intent to stay.

Additionally, there is abundant literature on **work-life spillover**, which is a within-person across-domains transmission of strain from one area of life to another, such as from work to home or from home to work. If an employee is struggling with mental health challenges and not getting the right help needed, even if the work environment wasn't the cause, this strain will still spill over into their work life and potentially impact their performance.

Be cautious around surveying employees about mental health challenges directly. Burnout signals may be a better choice when it comes to surveys. Ultimately, managers are not licensed mental healthcare professionals, but it is up to them to create a safe environment where those who are struggling feel comfortable sharing and seeking the needed support from work. If an employee discloses they were struggling, the manager can offer support by giving them time-off, for instance.

Additional education can also be helpful. Some organizations started to offer mental health first-aid training to managers during the COVID-19 pandemic. It is helpful for managers to be able to recognize the signs of struggles.

Developing Trauma-informed Leaders

Did you know that people who have experienced trauma in childhood are more likely to develop mental health challenges? I am not advocating for managers to take on roles of a therapist, but similar to how managers would notice their team member having a broken arm, it's helpful for managers to recognize signs of trauma. Here are some ways for organizations to get started.

Understanding the Impact of Trauma

Leaders need to get a handle on what trauma is and how it affects people. This means understanding different types of trauma, like childhood adversity, natural disasters, or community violence, and how it can show up in the workplace. It's about acknowledging that employees might be carrying some baggage from their past and that this can influence how they communicate and handle stress at work. Rather than blaming employees for their reactions, managers can be more understanding and listen with curiosity instead of judgment.

Adapting Leadership Practices

It's all about creating a workplace where everyone feels safe and supported. With Gen Z and millennial employees more openly discussing mental health challenges, including past trauma, managers need to model new behaviors, showing empathy, respect, and a nonjudgmental attitude. This creates a space where employees, regardless of background, can feel comfortable sharing their experiences and asking for help.

Leaders should also encourage self-care and remind employees to use resources the company offers, including EAP or health and fitness subsidies. Moreover, leaders should be aware of potential triggers in the workplace, like sudden organizational changes or conflict for certain team members, and know how to respond appropriately. These practices create a more supportive environment that promotes mental health.

Continuous Learning and Evaluation

Like everything else, trauma-informed leadership is an ongoing journey. The organization needs to gather feedback from employees and leaders to see what's working and what needs improvement on a regular basis. Survey and focus groups are potential ways to collect such data. This helps ensure that trauma-informed practices are truly effective and allow the organization to continuously improve its mental health support systems.

While I am not an expert on trauma, I understand it to be a very complex issue for anyone who has experienced it. Learning about how to talk about trauma and how it shows up for individuals sends a message to employees that their mental health is prioritized.

Senior leaders have the choice to remove stigma around mental health by encouraging employees to use related benefits. I've also seen how powerful it is when a senior leader shares their own mental health journey.

Speaking openly about mental health challenges isn't as modern as you might think. Churchill spoke openly about his depression and went through a particularly severe period in the years before the First World War: "For two or three years, the light faded from the picture. I did my work. I sat in the House of Commons. But a black depression settled on me,"[11] he later told his doctor.

Given the prevalence of mental health conditions, it's time organizations start being more supportive and compassionate about something that affects one in four people at some point in their lives.[12]

The Role of Age

Different groups will experience their own unique challenges on different aspects of well-being. Age plays a role in health conditions that impact different groups, such as menopause for women. Is it the organization's responsibility to create special policies for women in certain age groups? I understand if you feel nervous about this idea. But consider this, Research by the Chartered Institute of Personnel and Development in the United Kingdom found that two-thirds (67%) of working women between the ages of 40 and 60 with experience of menopausal symptoms said it had a mostly negative impact on them at work.[13] Of those who were negatively affected at work,

- 79% said they were less able to concentrate;
- 68% said they experienced more stress;
- nearly half (49%) said they felt less patient with clients and colleagues; and
- 46% felt less physically able to carry out work tasks.

As a result of this, more than half of respondents missed work due to their menopause symptoms.

Organizations across the globe are starting to have more open discussions around this topic, including creating a menopause workplace policy.

All Eyes on Gen Z

Another group of employees making the news is Gen Z. Being one of the most diverse generations, Gen Z wants its employers to place high value on diversity and representation in the workplace.

According to Roberta Katz, a former senior research scholar at Stanford's Center for Advanced Study in the Behavioral Sciences (CASBS), there are multiple ways Gen Z's preferences are changing the workforce. One of them being Gen Z's focus on mental health and work-life balance.

Being digital natives, Gen Z grew up in a period that saw the blurring of the 9-to-5 work schedule and the rise of flexible work models—a mode of working that led to older generations feeling a pressure to always be "on."

"Work and home life are all so integrated that if you don't pay attention, you could be working all the time," said Katz. "I think Gen Z is sensitive to that."

Having a work-life balance and maintaining mental and physical health is also important to Gen Z. "They're placing a value on the human experience and recognizing that life is more than work," Katz said.[14]

The Young Adults and Workplace Wellness Survey conducted by Georgetown University in partnership with Bank of America showed that to attract and retain Gen Z and young millennials, companies need to create a culture that celebrates wellness and fosters inclusion, professional advancement and success, as well as an overall sense of caring.[15]

This survey examines attitudes and priorities of 1,032 working-age Gen Z and younger millennials (ages 24–35). The responses show young adults overwhelmingly cite increased pay or compensation as the most critical factor both in deciding whether to remain with their current employer (73%) or in considering new employment (68%). Opportunities for promotion or growth, a more flexible work schedule, additional or better-quality benefits, and culture/values, in that order, rank next in importance when considering an employer. A more flexible work schedule or environment, in particular, is a much more significant factor in considering a move to another employer than in remaining with the current employer (49% and 38%, respectively), and even more so for women than men (54% of female young adults versus 44% of male young adults). Fewer than one in three young adults (32%) consider alignment of an employer's culture/values with their own to be a significant factor when thinking about new employment, and only one in four young adults (25%) find cultural alignment important in deciding whether to remain with their own employer.

The Gen Z and millennial struggle with work stress is documented in numerous surveys, including the Young Adults and Workplace Wellness Survey. Almost one-half (46%) of young adults indicate that they find it difficult to manage the stress of work and other things going on in their life (15% strongly agree). Those who are managing work stress well are more likely to say they feel cared about by their managers, have opportunities to grow, and the company has structures and policies in place to support work-life balance. While more than two in three young adults (68%) agree that their manager and other leaders at work make them feel like they care about them as a person, less than one in three young adults (30%) strongly agree with the statement. Furthermore, four in 10 young adults say their workplace always or sometimes feels toxic.

These numbers may be alarming to you. In the world of data, it's best to run your own survey rather than assuming that Gen Z and millennials want the same things as indicated in these surveys. Then you can leverage the power of AI to personalize experiences for different segments of employees based on the analysis. While it still needs to keep equity in check, there can be ways to include options that ensure equity but meet the needs of different groups.

Right to Disconnect

The drastic switch to remote working during the pandemic has made the line between home life and working hours unclear. Many employees feel they need to be available at all times via email, chat, text, and other channels. We know that answering calls and messages after office hours are over can lead to stress and burnout. Several countries across the globe have put legislation in place to protect the employees' "right to disconnect."

The European Union (EU) defines the right to disconnect as "a worker's right to be able to disengage from work and refrain from engaging in work-related electronic communications, such as emails or other messages, during non-work hours."[16]

This follows moves by several member states to establish legal precedents. France, seen by many as the pioneer in this area, enacted legislation in August 2016 allowing employees to switch off phones and other devices outside of set working hours.[17] Companies with 50+ employees are obliged to draw up a "charter of good conduct" setting specific hours when staff can't send or receive emails.

Portugal labels its work-life balance legislation the "right to rest," with companies of 10 or more staff facing fines for contacting staff outside of set working hours.[18] Workers with children below the age of eight are also permitted to work remotely under the new laws, which came into effect in November 2021.

Belgium passed a law in February 2022 allowing civil servants to switch off work emails, texts, and phone calls received out of hours, without fear of reprisals. The legislation protects the country's 65,000 public-sector employees from exposure to being permanently on-call, although out-of-hours contact is permissible in exceptional circumstances.

Australia's new legal right to disconnect allows workers to switch off after hours and choose not to engage with work communications.[19] This doesn't prevent employees from putting in additional hours, but it ensures they have the right to disconnect from "unreasonable contact" outside of designated working hours.

The legislation outlines factors to consider when determining whether contact outside working hours is reasonable, including the following:

- The nature and urgency of the reason for contact
- The method of contact (e.g., a phone call would likely be considered more disruptive than an email)
- Whether employees are compensated for working outside of their ordinary hours
- The level of the employee's responsibility within the organization
- The employee's personal circumstances

The United States doesn't currently have a similar law, but the California State Legislature recently introduced a bill designed to ensure employees are permitted to ignore emails, text messages, and phone calls from their employers during nonwork hours. The proposed bill, AB 2751 authored by Assembly member Matt Haney, would "require a public or private employer to establish a workplace policy that provides employees the right to disconnect from communications from the employer during nonworking hours" unless certain exceptions are met.

Although the bill is still in the early stages of the legislative process, the intent behind the proposed law is straightforward: California employees would have the right to completely disconnect from work outside their standard working hours. The bill would require employers to establish nonworking hours by written agreement with employees.[20]

Synchronize DEI and Well-being Strategies

Now that we have covered the link between DEI and well-being, how should you think about creating strategies that improve both outcomes?

- Getting the leaders together is easier said than done, especially when DEI and well-being leaders have separate budgets and teams.
- Developing inclusive well-being programs that address the needs of diverse employee groups will require tailored rather than one-size-fits-all messaging.

In the organizations I've worked with, the DEI programs often consist of **attract, retain,** and **develop** pillars. Can you design well-being programs to complement these pillars?

Well-being programs are often designed around different aspects, including **emotional, physical, financial,** and **social** well-being.

While all four pillars of well-being are important, one can argue that financial well-being is most important to job candidates considering your organizations as well as those who are debating whether or not to stay. One program design option is to focus on two aspects of well-being in each of the DEI program pillars. Figure 3.1 illustrates an example of how an interconnected program can look.

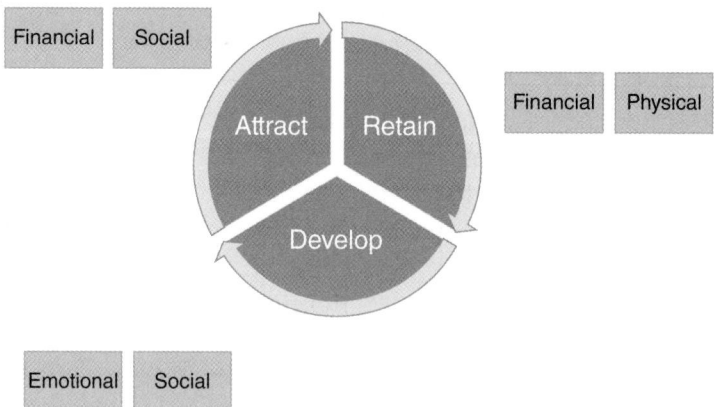

Figure 3.1   Sample Interconnected DEI and Well-being Program Design

Alternatively, you can thread all four aspects of well-being in each of the DEI pillars. Create a calendar for the year where each month the joint program of DEI and well-being focuses on one of the themes, such as how to improve emotional well-being in talent development, or how to improve social well-being for top performers we want to retain.

Here's a 12-month calendar example for inspiration:

- Month 1: "New Year, New You"—Well-being + DEI Program
  - Program Title: "Embracing Diversity and Setting Intentions"
  - Description: Kick off the new year with a program that combines setting personal well-being intentions with diversity and inclusion goals. Employees will participate in a guided meditation and reflection exercise to set intentions for the year, followed by a diversity and inclusion workshop on the importance of embracing diversity and promoting inclusion in the workplace.
- Month 2: "Love Is Love"—Well-being + DEI Program
  - Program Title: "Building Inclusive Relationships"
  - Description: Celebrate Valentine's Day with a program that focuses on building inclusive relationships and promoting emotional well-being. Employees will participate in a workshop on building inclusive relationships, followed by a guided meditation on self-love and self-acceptance.
- Month 3: "Women's History Month"—Well-being + DEI Program
  - Program Title: "Empowering Women, Empowering Well-being"
  - Description: Celebrate Women's History Month with a program that empowers women and promotes physical well-being. Employees will participate in a fitness class focused on women's empowerment, followed by a workshop on gender equity and inclusion in the workplace.
- Month 4: "Mental Health Awareness Month"—Well-being + DEI Program
  - Program Title: "Breaking Down Barriers to Mental Health"
  - Description: Celebrate Mental Health Awareness Month with a program that breaks down barriers to mental health and

promotes emotional well-being. Employees will participate in a workshop on mental health and bias, followed by a guided meditation on stress reduction and resilience.

- Month 5: "Asian American and Pacific Islander Heritage Month"—Well-being + DEI Program
  - Program Title: "Celebrating Cultural Heritage and Financial Well-being"
  - Description: Celebrate Asian American and Pacific Islander Heritage Month with a program that promotes financial well-being and celebrates cultural heritage. Employees will participate in a workshop on financial planning and wealth management, followed by a cultural celebration and networking event.
- Month 6: "Pride Month"—Well-being + DEI Program
  - Program Title: "Pride and Progress: Promoting LGBTQ+ Inclusion and Well-being"
  - Description: Celebrate Pride Month with a program that promotes LGBTQ+ inclusion and well-being. Employees will participate in a workshop on LGBTQ+ inclusion and allyship, followed by a guided meditation on self-acceptance and self-love.
- Month 7: "Disability Independence Day"—Well-being + DEI Program
  - Program Title: "Accessibility and Inclusion: Promoting Disability Awareness and Well-being"
  - Description: Celebrate Disability Independence Day with a program that promotes disability awareness and well-being. Employees will participate in a workshop on disability inclusion and accessibility, followed by a fitness class focused on adaptive fitness.
- Month 8: "Black Business Month"—Well-being + DEI Program
  - Program Title: "Empowering Black Entrepreneurs and Promoting Financial Well-being"
  - Description: Celebrate Black Business Month with a program that empowers Black entrepreneurs and promotes financial well-being. Employees will participate in a workshop on

financial planning and entrepreneurship, followed by a networking event for Black entrepreneurs.

- Month 9: "Hispanic Heritage Month"—Well-being + DEI Program
  - Program Title: "Celebrating Hispanic Heritage and Promoting Social Well-being"
  - Description: Celebrate Hispanic Heritage Month with a program that promotes social well-being and celebrates cultural heritage. Employees will participate in a workshop on building inclusive relationships, followed by a cultural celebration and networking event.
- Month 10: "Mental Illness Awareness Week"—Well-being + DEI Program
  - Program Title: "Breaking Down Barriers to Mental Health and Promoting Emotional Well-being"
  - Description: Celebrate Mental Illness Awareness Week with a program that breaks down barriers to mental health and promotes emotional well-being. Employees will participate in a workshop on mental health and bias, followed by a guided meditation on stress reduction and resilience.
- Month 11: "Native American Heritage Month"—Well-being + DEI Program
  - Program Title: "Honoring Native American Heritage and Promoting Physical Well-being"
  - Description: Celebrate Native American Heritage Month with a program that promotes physical well-being and honors cultural heritage. Employees will participate in a fitness class focused on Native American cultural dances, followed by a cultural celebration and networking event.
- Month 12: "Year-End Reflection and Goal Setting"—Well-being + DEI Program
  - Program Title: "Reflecting on Diversity and Inclusion Goals and Setting Intentions for the New Year"
  - Description: End the year with a program that reflects on diversity and inclusion goals and sets intentions for the new year. Employees will participate in a guided meditation and

Month	Theme	DEI Pillar	Well-being Pillar
January	Inclusive Hiring & Onboarding	Attract	Financial
February	Building a Culture of Allyship	Develop	Emotional

Figure 3.2 Synchronized Program Planning Calendar

reflection exercise to set intentions for the year, followed by a workshop on diversity and inclusion goals and strategies for the new year.

Remember: This calendar is a starting point. Adapt and adjust programs based on employee needs and organizational goals. By integrating DEI and well-being efforts, organizations can create a more inclusive, supportive, and thriving workplace that attracts, retains, and develops a diverse and engaged workforce.

Figure 3.2 shows an alternative format for a synchronized program planning calendar, which you can tailor to your organization.

Organization Structure: Should You Merge DEI and Well-being?

I recall hearing a discussion around combining DEI and well-being into a single function at an event. If this seems unfathomable, you are not alone.

Would you be surprised if I told you these roles exist today?

A search on LinkedIn for "Head of DEI and Well-being" returned only two results but "Head of inclusion and well-being" returned more than 40 results for current employees. Figure 3.3 shows the results of these searches, which are much smaller than the number of head of well-being and head of diversity or DEI roles. Figure 3.4 shows these results for comparison purposes.

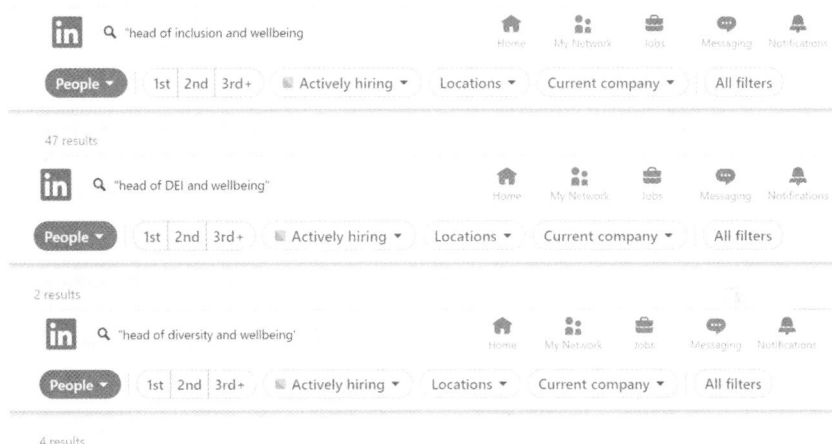

Figure 3.3   LinkedIn Search Results for Combined Head of Inclusion and Well-being Roles

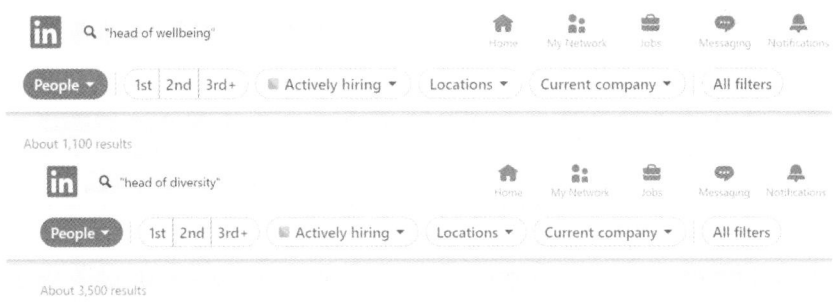

Figure 3.4   LinkedIn Search Results for Head of Well-being and DEI Roles Separately

What would a combined role look like in terms of job responsibilities and skills? From an example of a job description for a "Head of Diversity and Well-being" in the United Kingdom, following are a summary of the role requirements.[21]

What you will do

- Lead DEI and Well-being Initiatives: Oversee the DE&I team to implement strategies that promote inclusivity.
- Engage with Senior Leaders: Collaborate with leadership to align on DE&I goals and ensure commitment.
- External Representation: Act as the voice of Sainsbury's on DE&I matters at external events and committees.
- Monitor Industry Trends: Stay informed about developments in DE&I and well-being to enhance organizational practices.
- Manage Reporting: Ensure timely delivery of DE&I and well-being reports and assessments.
- Support Employee Resource Groups: Optimize the role of internal networks in supporting colleagues.
- Feedback and Improvement: Gather qualitative and quantitative feedback to refine strategies and programs.

What you need to know and show:

- Strategic Leadership: Ability to develop and implement diversity, equity, inclusion (DE&I), and well-being strategies.
- Stakeholder Management: Experience engaging with senior leaders and managing relationships up to Operating Board level.
- Data-Driven Decision-making: Proficiency in using data and metrics to drive improvements and measure progress.
- Communication Skills: Strong written and verbal abilities to influence and advocate for DE&I initiatives.
- Change Management: Track record of driving organizational change and fostering an inclusive culture.
- Empathy and Creativity: Ability to understand diverse perspectives and develop innovative solutions.
- Deep Domain Knowledge: Deep understanding of DEI and well-being agendas. Extensive knowledge of best practices and trends in diversity, equity, inclusion, and well-being.

Most of the skills listed such as data-driven decision-making and stakeholder management are high transferable skills. However, a deep expertise of both DEI and well-being may be more difficult to find within one candidate given these practices sit in silos in most organizations.

Should you combine the roles? While there's no one-size-fits-all answer, it's helpful to consider both options.

Combining the DEI and well-being roles can have its advantages. For one, it allows for a more holistic approach to employee experience, recognizing that DEI are intricately linked to overall well-being for every employee. A single leader can oversee both areas, ensuring a more cohesive strategy and reducing silos that would normally exist. More importantly, combining roles can help streamline resources and budget allocations, making it easier to allocate funds to the most critical initiatives.

On the other hand, keeping DEI and well-being separate allows each area to receive the specialized attention it deserves from leaders with deep expertise in each. DEI initiatives often require a deep understanding of systemic inequalities and cultural nuances, while well-being initiatives demand experience in workplace mental health, ergonomics, and benefits design. Separating the two roles ensures that each area has a leader who can drive meaningful change and make progress.

Regardless of whether the roles are combined or separate, it's critical that the leaders of DEI and well-being work together in a proactive manner. This collaboration can lead to innovative solutions that address the complex needs of employees. For instance, a well-being initiative focused on mental health can be informed by DEI principles to ensure that programs are accessible and effective for all employees. The CEO and CHRO should incentivize open communication and collaboration between DEI and well-being leaders to ensure a cohesive approach to employee experience.

When it comes to budgeting, the decision to combine or separate funds will depend on multiple factors, including the organization's size, industry, decision-making process, and business priorities. However, reviewing the 12-month calendar can provide valuable insights into what to bring to the C-suite for the next budget conversation. By examining the timing of DEI and well-being initiatives, leaders can identify opportunities for cost-sharing and resource optimization to improve overall employee experience. The CFO should analyze budget allocations and identify opportunities for cost-sharing and resource optimization.

Overall, the decision to combine or separate DEI and well-being roles depends on a complex list of factors. By understanding the advantages and disadvantages of each approach, organizations can make informed decisions that support the overall well-being and success of their employees.

A Discussion on Neurodiversity, Disability, and Accessibility

One particular area gaining attention is neurodivergent employees. Why are they important to your business? An estimated 15% or more people are neurodivergent, so it's more than likely that you will work with a neurodivergent colleague.

Neurodivergent individuals, with their unique ways of thinking, bring innovative perspectives to problems in your organization. Here are some ways you can tap into their strengths:

- **Creative Solutions:** Neurodivergent employees often excel at thinking outside the box, finding creative solutions to complex problems, and identifying patterns others may miss.
- **Detail Oriented:** Their attention to detail can be a huge advantage in different situations, ensuring accuracy and quality in the business.
- **Mirroring the Customers:** A workforce that includes neurodivergent individuals, reflects the diversity of the company's customer base, which can ultimately improve the products and services.

Supporting neurodivergent employees is key to maximizing their unique talents. You can tailor to their individual needs and create a neuro-inclusive workplace by doing the following:

- **Environment Matters:** Noise, light, and desk setup can impact focus and productivity. Consider quiet spaces, adjustable lighting, and ergonomic equipment.
- **Flexibility Is Key:** Offer flexible work arrangements that cater to individual needs, allowing employees to thrive in their own way.
- **Listen and Learn:** Engage with neurodivergent individuals to understand their specific challenges and create solutions that truly work.

By embracing neurodiversity, you'll be able to tap into talent and creativity that can propel your business forward.

Another dimension of diversity is disability. According to the United Nations data, 80% to 90% of persons with disabilities of working age in developing countries are unemployed, whereas in industrialized countries the figure is between 50% and 70%.[22]

A report by the US Bureau of Labor Statistics states, only 19.1% of people with disabilities are employed.[23] However, disability discrimination is one of the most commonly reported types of employment discrimination—with nearly 25,000 claims filed across the United States in 2020.[24]

Not all disabilities are visible and apparent. In addition to making sure accessibility can be achieved with ramps and accessible restrooms, organizations must ensure accessibility for all employees, including those with invisible disabilities, such as post-traumatic stress disorder (PTSD) or HIV.

It may be difficult for employees with invisible disabilities to request accommodations if it's not easy to know how others with the same disability are treated. While we can see whether there is a ramp for wheelchair entrance to the office building, we can't see what accommodations are provided to employees who suffer from PTSD.

Organizations can implement several practices to support people with invisible or nonapparent disabilities:

- Create a work environment where employees with a nonapparent disability would feel comfortable disclosing their status if necessary. Employers should have plenty of resources for employees to express their access needs **anonymously.**

- Establish employee resource groups aimed at improving accessibility in the workplace. These groups can help provide a supportive space for individuals to ask questions and get additional help.
- Ensure health plans include coverage that could help employees with nonapparent disabilities get health insurance through work.

GenAI Applications: Inclusion and Well-being as an Integrated Effort

Here are some ways GenAI can improve both employee well-being and inclusion as intertwined aspects of a thriving workplace:

- **Personalized Onboarding:** GenAI can create customized onboarding experiences that cater to individual needs and preferences, fostering a sense of belonging from day one. It can analyze employee data (demographics, interests, skills) to tailor welcome messages, training materials, and mentorship programs.
- **Inclusive Communication:** GenAI can analyze communication patterns within the organization to identify potential biases and suggest more inclusive language. It can also help create diverse and representative content for internal newsletters, company announcements, and social media, ensuring everyone feels seen and heard.
- **Inclusive and Thriving Team Formation:** GenAI can analyze employee skills, interests, and communication styles to suggest project teams that are more diverse and inclusive. While formal team structures in organizations are typically determined based on a different process, it can be potentially useful to analyze current team makeup to see if individuals from different backgrounds and perspectives are included on a team.
- **Data Visualization:** We cover storytelling at length in the prior chapter. You can leverage GenAI to create interactive dashboards and visualizations to track progress on both DEI and well-being

initiatives in one place. This allows organizations to understand the impact of their efforts and identify areas for improvement.

Given the risks, there are also times when GenAI should be off-limits. Here is when and how not to use GenAI:

- **The tendency to hallucinate.** Don't treat GenAI as an expert due to the known hallucination problems. Remember, GenAI cannot think. It doesn't understand what you are writing even though it acts like it. It's simply guessing the next word and the word after that.
- **Data privacy and security issues.** Don't upload anything to ChatGPT or other foundational models that you don't want the world to see. In fact, if you are not sure about the data privacy and security, I'd recommend proceeding as if the world will see what you've uploaded.
- **Lack of human oversight.** Don't send AI to make a decision without humans involved. At its present state, GenAI should not be left to make talent decisions without any human judgment. While human judgment has its own biases and issues, GenAI could make these biases worse.

A Brief Note on Correlation Versus Causation

You've likely heard at some point in your life that correlation isn't causation. It is crucial to distinguish between the two concepts, especially in workplace research where conflating these ideas can lead to misleading conclusions and strategies.

Correlation refers to the statistical relationship between variables. Specifically, correlation measures the extent to which changes in one variable are associated with changes in another variable. The most commonly used measure of correlation is the Pearson correlation coefficient (ρ), which ranges from -1 (perfect negative correlation) to 1 (perfect positive correlation), with 0 indicating no correlation.

Suppose we collect data on ice cream sales and weather in your city over the past two years. We might observe a strong positive correlation between ice cream sales and warm weather, indicating that as temperature increases, ice cream sales also tend to increase. However, this correlation does not necessarily imply that temperature causes ice cream sales to rise. Nor would one conclude that ice cream sale causes the temperature to increase. This is an example that most of us can relate to. What about well-being and inclusion? Do higher inclusion levels cause well-being to increase? Or does feeling well cause the sense of inclusion? We know the two factors are related, but is there a causal relationship?

What is causation? Causation refers to the cause-and-effect relationship between variables. In other words, causation implies that a change in one variable leads to a change in another variable. Causation is a key concept that allows researchers to make informed decisions and recommendations.

Imagine you're studying the relationship between flexible work arrangements and employee well-being. You collect data on the number of employees who are allowed to work from home three days a week and their subsequent self-reported well-being scores.

You first notice that employees who are allowed to work from home three days a week tend to have higher well-being scores than those who are not. In fact, the data shows a strong positive correlation between having this flexibility and their self-reported well-being.

Does this mean allowing employees to work from home **causes** an increase in their well-being? It's tempting to conclude that flexible work arrangements cause an increase in employee well-being. After all, the data show a strong correlation between the two variables. But before we jump to conclusions, we have to explore alternative explanations. For example, is it possible that employees who are more productive and efficient are more likely to be granted flexible work arrangements, which in turn affects their well-being?

Is it possible that employees who have better work-life balance to begin with are more likely to be granted flexible work arrangements, which affects their well-being?

Or perhaps there's a third factor, such as job autonomy, that affects both flexible work arrangements and employee well-being.

Any of these possibilities would "pollute" the simple conclusion of flexible work causes well-being to increase. While this can be challenging, it's vital to figure out the direction of causation if we want to create data-informed strategies.

In this chapter, we discussed the interconnectedness of well-being and inclusion in the workplace. We also covered the role of demographic characteristics such as race and age in well-being. Age plays a pivotal role in employee well-being, with distinct groups facing unique challenges. Organizations must address age-related issues, such as menopause policies for women and work-life balance for Gen Z, to attract and retain a diverse workforce.

Employers must also be mindful of the mental healthcare access disparity between groups, as social determinants of health, including transportation barriers, discrimination, income disparities, and language barriers. To address this, organizations should collect quantitative and qualitative data on well-being program usage across different employee demographics, identify factors contributing to disparities, and develop targeted interventions to ensure equitable access to mental health resources for all employees.

We also discuss how to leverage AI to personalize experiences for different segments of employees based on data analysis. By designing synchronized programs that recognize the strong connection between well-being and inclusion, and addressing the disparities in mental healthcare access, organizations can create a healthier and more productive workforce.

The next chapter will dive into how to quantify the impact of DEI and well-being initiatives on outcomes.

Notes

1. American Psychological Association. (2023). *2023 work in America survey.* Apa.org. Available at: https://www.apa.org/pubs/reports/work-in-america/2023-workplace-health-well-being

2. Vance, T.A. (2019). *Addressing mental health in the Black community.* Columbia University Department of Psychiatry. Available at: https://www.columbiapsychiatry.org/news/addressing-mental-health-black-community

3. CARE. (2020). *Rapid gender analysis: Filling the data gap to build back equal.* Available at: https://www.care.org/wp-content/uploads/2020/09/RGA_SheToldUsSo_9.18.20.pdf

4. Ridley, M., Rao, G., Schilbach, F., and Patel, V. (2020). Poverty, depression, and anxiety: causal evidence and mechanisms. *Science* [online]. 370(6522), p.1. doi: https://doi.org/10.1126/science.aay0214

5. Sprc.org. (2015). *Racial/ethnic differences in mental health service use among adults—Suicide Prevention Resource Center.* [online] Available at: https://sprc.org/online-library/racial-ethnic-differences-in-mental-health-service-use-among-adults/ [Accessed 3 Nov. 2024].

6. Lin, L., Stamm, K., and Christidis, P. (2018). How diverse is the psychology workforce? *American Psychological Association.* Available at: https://www.apa.org/monitor/2018/02/datapoint

7. Deloitte. (2024). *Uncovering culture: A call to action for leaders.* Available at: https://www2.deloitte.com/us/en/pages/about-deloitte/articles/uncovering-culture.html

8. Thehartford.com. (2019). *The Hartford's new study: Black US workers face greater barriers to mental health support at work* [online]. Available at: https://newsroom.thehartford.com/newsroom-home/news-releases/news-releases-details/2023/The-Hartfords-New-Study-Black-U.S.-Workers-Face-Greater-Barriers-To-Mental-Health-Support-At-Work/default.aspx

9. Yamkovenko, B. and Tavares, S. (2017). To understand whether your company is inclusive, map how your employees interact. *Harvard Business Review.* Available at: https://hbr.org/2017/07/to-understand-whether-your-company-is-inclusive-map-how-your-employees-interact

10. Textio. (2024). *2024 Language bias in performance feedback.* Available at: https://textio.com/feedback-bias-2024

11. Thomson, S. (2015). *4 great leaders who had mental health problems* [online]. World Economic Forum. Available at: https://www.weforum.org/agenda/2015/10/4-great-leaders-who-had-mental-health-problems/

12. World Health Organization. (2001). *Mental disorders affect one in four people* [online]. Available at: `http://www.who.int/whr/2001/media_centre/press_release/en/`

13. CIPD. (2023). *Menopause in the workplace* [online]. Available at: `https://www.cipd.org/uk/knowledge/reports/menopause-workplace-experiences/`

14. De Witte, M. (2024). *8 ways Gen Z will change the workforce* [online]. news.stanford.edu. Available at: `https://news.stanford.edu/stories/2024/02/8-things-expect-gen-z-coworker`

15. Krause, S. (2023). *New research explores how millennials and Gen Z are driving a new definition of workplace wellness—McDonough School of Business* [online]. Available at: `https://msb.georgetown.edu/news-story/research-and-insights/new-research-explores-how-millennials-and-gen-z-are-driving-a-new-definition-of-workplace-wellness/` [accessed 3 Nov 2024].

16. Eurofound. (2021). *Right to disconnect* [online]. Available at: `https://www.eurofound.europa.eu/observatories/eurwork/industrial-relations-dictionary/right-to-disconnect`

17. French workers get 'right to disconnect' from emails out of hours. (2016). *BBC News*. 31 Dec. Available at: `https://www.bbc.co.uk/news/world-europe-38479439`

18. Portugal bans bosses texting staff after-hours. (2021). *BBC News*. 12 Nov. Available at: `https://www.bbc.com/news/business-59263300`

19. *Fair Work Amendment Bill 2024*. www.aph.gov.au. Available at: `https://www.aph.gov.au/Parliamentary_Business/Bills_Legislation/bd/bd2324a/24bd052`

20. Marr, C. and Oxford, A. (2024). *'Right to disconnect' plan in California hits employer backlash*. Available at: `https://news.bloomberglaw.com/daily-labor-report/right-to-disconnect-plan-in-california-hits-employer-backlash`

21. *Sainsbury's Head of Diversity and Wellbeing*. (n.d.). Talentify. Available at: `https://www.talentify.io/job/head-of-dei-and-well-being-london-england-sainsburys-228792` [accessed Nov 4, 2024]

22. United Nations. (2019). *Disability and employment*. Un.org. Available at: `https://www.un.org/development/desa/disabilities/resources/factsheet-on-persons-with-disabilities/disability-and-employment.html`

23. Bureau of Labor Statistics. (2024). *Persons with a disability: Labor Force Characteristics.* Available at: https://www.bls.gov/news.release/pdf/disabl.pdf

24. U.S. Equal Employment Opportunity Commission. (2023). *Enforcement and litigation statistics.* US EEOC. Available at: https://www.eeoc.gov/data/enforcement-and-litigation-statistics-0

Chapter 4

Quantify the ROI of DEI and Well-being Programs

ERGs are not just nice-to-have programs. We have hard data to show that ERG participation improves the career outcomes for individual employees and that drives overall business success.
– Lani Hall, Global Diversity and Inclusion Leader

Business leaders are responsible for demonstrating how each function contributes substantial value to the organization. Investments in DEI and well-being are no exception. It is essential to clearly connect these initiatives to the bottom line. This chapter presents proven methods for measuring the return on investment (ROI) in ways that resonate with finance and provides real-world case studies based on interviews with practitioners.

Program Evaluation Fundamentals

Every year, without fail, my inbox received a few emails with a familiar query: "Can you help quantify the ROI of this program?" These emails, often from department heads or HR leaders, carried the weight of executive scrutiny. They read, "The CFO wants to know the ROI on the new training program," or "The CEO wants to know the ROI on the meditation app we implemented."

I adopted a three-step approach, shown in Figure 4.1, that helped me respond to these requests effectively.

The first step was always to determine the specific metric the program intended to improve. This could range from employee retention rates to productivity levels to promotion rates.

Once the metric was identified, the next step was to quantify the impact of the change in that metric post-program implementation. This involved collecting data before and after the program's launch, analyzing trends, and isolating the program's effect from other variables. The goal was to present a clear story that demonstrated how the program impacted the metric of choice.

Sometimes there are too many other factors that can contribute to metrics like retention, and organizations choose to demonstrate impact with post-program surveys instead. At Kraft Heinz, for instance, the company Speaker series has a post-event evaluation designed to gauge behavior change through effectiveness and value. "For value, 100% of participants agreed that the learning experience was a valuable use of their time. For effectiveness and business impact, 94% agreed that they gained insights from the experience that will impact their job performance."[1]

The final step was calculating the net return on investment. This was done by subtracting the cost of the program from the financial impact of the change in the identified metric. Let's walk

Figure 4.1 Three-step Process of ROI Quantification

through an example that frequently surfaced in these discussions: an inclusion training for managers.

An Example: Inclusive Management Training

Consider a training program designed to enhance inclusive management practices with the aim of improving the retention of diverse talent. The process began with establishing a baseline for employee turnover rates, particularly among diverse groups. After the training program was conducted, we monitored the turnover rates over the next several months.

Let's assume the training program costs $100,000. Post-training, we observed a 10% reduction in turnover among diverse employees. If the average cost of replacing an employee is $50,000, and the company loses 20 diverse employees per year historically, the annual turnover cost is $1,000,000. A 10% reduction translates to retaining two more employees, saving $100,000 annually.

The net ROI calculation would be straightforward:

- **Financial Impact:** $100,000 (cost savings from reduced turnover)
- **Program Cost**: $100,000
- **Net ROI:** $100,000 – $100,000 = $0 (breaking even, but potentially higher savings over multiple years)

You can also use this calculation to determine beforehand what the break-even number is and use it for target setting. It is also helpful to apply the calculation in pilot programs before rolling out to the entire organization. If the net ROI is not positive within a reasonable time frame, consider revamping or sunsetting the program.

This example highlights a lesson I saw in the interviews I conducted: the importance of aligning any initiatives with financial outcomes. Several leaders shared in our conversations that their CEO or CFO would simply not accept proposals without a clear ROI within 6–12 months. Quantifying ROI is not merely an exercise in number-crunching, it is also how these leaders are able to expand their teams and increase their impact.

A Discussion on Employee Resource Groups

The first official employee resource group (ERG) in the United States, the Xerox National Black Employees Caucus, was created in 1970 as a forum for Black employees to advocate for inclusion and change within the company. Does it work? An estimated 90% of Fortune 500 companies have ERGs.[2]

The dimensions of effectiveness can include career advancement, community building, connection or visibility to leadership, allyship, sense of inclusion and belonging, and overall well-being.

Applying this methodology, the first step is to align with stakeholders on the measurement of effectiveness or impact. In this case, the stakeholders should include the head of DEI and the C-level leaders funding ERGs at the minimum. The CEO and CFO are often involved in F500 DEI initiatives as key sponsors as well and having a clear measurement methodology goes a long way.

There are a few considerations when it comes to ERGs in companies. Following are important questions to discuss and align on:

- How will we as a company reward and recognize ERG-related time and efforts, whether it's the formal leadership roles of ERG or contributions such as being a speaker at ERG events?
- How will we provide financial support to ERGs and what is the ROI requirement for continued funding? Will we have C-suite executives aligned with each of the ERGs as champions? How will the budget for each ERG be determined? Will we have cross-ERG initiatives as well? If so, what is the purpose, and who will sponsor these?
- How will we ensure the ERG strategies connect with the overall company DEI strategy? What roles will DEI leadership, HR leadership, ERG leadership, and C-suite champions play in these strategy conversations?

I've seen conflict arise between corporate DEI teams and ERGs due to misalignment on the strategy and purpose. Effective DEI leadership teams host annual and quarterly meetings to share their strategies with ERGs so the groups can devote proper resources to overall DEI strategy.

I recall heated debates about whether to compensate the ERG leaders years ago. While it started out as service work, many ERG leaders find that the work demands a large amount of their time. There need to be rewards and recognition for ERG leadership for long-term sustainability. It would be helpful for the company leadership to first align on the goals and purpose of ERGs and how to reward employees who step up to lead these organizations.

Having strong executive support is also critical for success of ERGs. You can have each C-level executive sponsor one ERG and centrally manage the budget for all groups. Some forecasting may be helpful as well so you know how large each ERG will be in the next 6, 12, 24, and 36 months. Start with what the ERGs will aim to accomplish, then allocate budget accordingly.

Leadership Program

Sometimes the data surprises you.

A few years ago, I was asked to evaluate the effectiveness of a leadership program for high-potential women. The talent development team poured their heart and soul into creating a six-month-long program for women who have the potential to become executives in the company. It was a highly selective and nomination-based cohort program.

Three cohorts later, we analyzed the data to gauge the return on investment. The program did indeed correlate with higher promotion rates for participants compared to nonparticipants. However, the retention data told a different story—the attrition rate was higher among those who completed the program, which was counterintuitive and disappointing initially. It was certainly bad news our talent development team didn't want to hear.

(continued)

(continued)

At first, the knee-jerk reaction was to try to poke holes in the data. "Maybe the data was wrong. Maybe there were confounding factors? Perhaps the sample size was too small?" After triple-checking the data and analysis, we didn't find any issues. As we dug deeper through interviews and focus groups, slowly some clear themes emerged from the qualitative data:

First, the program itself was extremely demanding on top of already high-pressure roles. While meaningful, it contributed to burnout that made some reevaluate their longevity here. As one participant told us: "The program made me realize how exhausted I really was and for years the only reward I got for doing great work was more work. I didn't want to live that life forever."

Second, the workshops and executive coaching gave women a new lens into their own potential that they hadn't quite seen before. As another participant put it: "My eyes were opened to new types of roles I could truly thrive with my new skills. And I realized those roles were not available within our organization."

Finally, the leadership training itself gave participants valuable skills that made them marketable inside and outside the organization. The company had invested in accelerating their development, as intended, but it was also a double-edged sword.

While some chose to stay and were promoted thanks to the program's impact, many took their expanded capabilities to an external opportunity they hadn't considered previously. The timing was also challenging for some participants. Given that executive roles were limited, not every participant who wanted to be promoted could get promoted right away, which prompted them to look externally.

One change we made based on the feedback was the amount of work from the program to ease the burden on participants. Another was to request the participants' manager to have more frequent check-ins as their team learned more about their own capabilities and aspirations.

In analyzing the data and hearing the "why" behind the numbers, the talent development team evolved their perspective. Higher attrition wasn't always bad—if it meant supporting talented leaders' growth. Even if not within our walls, it could still be considered success with a broader definition. Sometimes the data surprises you by showing there's more than one way to view your objectives.

As part of the research for this book, I had the privilege of interviewing numerous leaders across DEI, workplace well-being, and people analytics domains. These conversations provided invaluable insights into the strategies and mindsets driving success in these areas. Several common themes emerged.

Running DEI and Well-being as a Business with Clear Metrics

One of the most remarkable findings from my interviews was the importance of running DEI and well-being initiatives as a strategic business function, rather than a mere feel-good exercise or one-time public relations stunt. The leaders who have seen the most significant impact consistently approach their work like the P&L owner rather than a master of execution. They set clear north stars for their functions, defining a measurement strategy so they know the progress over time.

"ERGs are not just nice-to-have programs. We have hard data to show that ERG participation improves the career outcomes for individual employees and that drives overall business success," said Lani Hall, Global Diversity and Inclusion Leader. "The company is data-driven so we treat our DEI strategy like any other critical business initiative, with defined objectives, KPIs, and regular reviews with executive leadership."

The traditional DEI and well-being measures, such as representation data and employee engagement scores, while important, do not tend to get the attention of the C-suite. That means it is difficult if not impossible to obtain funding for these programs. The most effective leaders go beyond these measures and connect with tangible business metrics such as absenteeism and productivity.

"I think we need to change the conversation around well-being to be focused on performance for the business so we can engage senior leaders, rather than talking about well-being as a fluffy concept," said Chris Cummings, founder of Wellbeing at Work. Speaking the business language matters. From the case studies Chris has seen across the globe, the two largest barriers to employee well-being are (1) the language we use hasn't been what the C-suite needs to hear and (2) not measuring, or measuring but not connecting, well-being metrics to business outcomes the C-suite cares about.

Focusing on Business Questions and Proactive Data Collection

Another common theme among the leaders I interviewed was a willingness to think beyond the constraints of existing data systems and proactively collect new information or come up with creative solutions as a proxy to answer critical business questions. I know firsthand what it's like to stare at the HR database and wonder why some important data elements are missing. Rather than being limited by what is available in the systems or what the legal team said was permissible, these leaders take a courageous and business-focused approach to identifying the data points that matter most and finding ethical, compliant ways to obtain them.

Dr. Alexis Fink, vice president of People Analytics and Workforce Strategy at Meta, said she combines qualitative and quantitative data in her work. "There is no replacement for qualitative when it comes to smaller samples, combined with personal and sensitive context." She continued, "Quantitative data helps you understand gives you answers to 'WHERE to dig,' and qualitative research helps you uncover nuances in meaning."

As a people analytics practitioner, I've had my fair share of tough conversations with legal and privacy stakeholders on the risks of capturing certain data elements. If I could offer my biggest learnings, it would be to never surprise your legal and privacy teams, and to bring them into the conversation as early as possible. Another lesson is to use storytelling skills to bring to life the benefits of collecting these additional data points. The legal and privacy teams tend to approach the data collection with a risk lens, so it is up to you to guide them to see a different perspective.

Shujaat Ahmad is one of the founding members of the People Analytics team at LinkedIn. He built a workforce representation mix model with inflow and outflow with scenario planning capability. The seemingly simple model brought insights on what it'll take to move the needle on diversity, which was critical at the time because many leaders assumed the numbers would change in a quarter or two.

"Diversity is a small data problem; we make the mistake of only applying a big data lens to it," said Shujaat. "The magic is in combining both."

The data-focused approach was helpful to challenge the convention that if 95% say a solution is working then we should move on, as some underserved groups make up less than 5% of the employee population. That 5% may have some of your top performing and most critical talent in critical roles but you would never know.

This proactive mindset extends to ERG leaders as well, with leaders pushing for more granular demographic data collection, voluntary self-identification campaigns, and transparency around data.

"The traditional demographic categories we capture in our HR systems don't provide enough nuance to understand the true diversity of our workforce and the unique experiences and challenges different Asian groups face," noted Carlo Dela Fuente of Cisco.

Recognizing the Strong Connection Between DEI and Well-being

While there is limited existing research on this topic, it is clear that top leaders recognize the intrinsic link between DEI and well-being in the workplace. The leaders who have seen the greatest success in both areas have adopted a more holistic approach and collaborate proactively with their counterparts.

Tashi Theisman, vice president of Global Benefits, said she has partnered closely with inclusion & diversity teams and ERGs. Her department implemented health programs for Black and Latino communities with respect to medical coverage because of different social determinants of health. ERGs help ensure different groups can get the help they need. Plus, ERGs provide a way for feedback gathering so they serve as another listening channel. This data gathering is particularly important before and after rolling out programs that are designed for specific groups such as women in tech or caregivers.

We intuitively know that employees from underrepresented or marginalized groups may face unique challenges, so addressing well-being without considering the DEI lens is an incomplete approach. This sentiment was echoed by many of the corporate leaders interviewed, who emphasized the importance of a sense of inclusion and belonging to well-being at work.

One thing that improved the well-being for employees from underrepresented groups is knowing where they stood in the organization. "Employees tell us there was a lot of anxiety around their career and future growth prior to having this level of transparency," said Lani Hall, chief diversity officer. In my conversation with Hall, I was suddenly reminded of being part of the high-potential programs at multiple companies yet I wasn't told until I asked explicitly why I was in the program. In fact, I felt anxious about the development and training I was about to receive because I assumed the reason for me being in the program was because I wasn't performing!

Lani and other corporate leaders I interviewed also shared their organization placed a strong emphasis on creating a psychologically safe and supportive environment for all employees. This was both measured via surveys and included as part of leadership or DEI trainings at their company.

At LinkedIn, the Black Inclusion Group (BIG) hosted a mental health check-in with Dr. Michael McRae, assistant commissioner of the Bureau of Health Promotion for Justice-Impacted Populations at the New York City Department of Health and Mental Hygiene. Embrace ERG, which celebrates individuals from all backgrounds, cultures, and nationalities hosted a virtual show-and-tell where employees shared family keepsakes and travel stories.[3] Events like this strengthened the connectivity tissue globally.

As these interviews have shown, the most successful leaders in DEI, well-being, and people analytics share a common mindset: a willingness to think bigger, challenge the status quo, and take a data-driven approach to achieve impact within their organizations. Ultimately, because these trailblazers are willing push the boundaries and take smart risks, their companies are able to create a truly inclusive and supportive environment for all employees.

Are Well-being Apps Worth the Cost?

During the COVID-19 pandemic, many companies invested in well-being apps, including Amanda's company. Since the company gym was closed in the pandemic and most employees were working remotely, the leadership team made a big investment in rolling out a new well-being app for employees. The app promised to help reduce burnout, increase mindfulness, and improve sleep quality—all crucial things during challenging times. The app had a user-friendly design and included features like guided meditations, sleep stories, and breathing exercises. The communications team worked with the implementation team to promote the app internally after the CEO and CHRO announced it. There were multiple education sessions for employees in each of the business units so everyone knew how to sign up for the free benefits. A few employees were very excited and shared how they loved the sleep stories for their toddlers at home.

But after several months, the HR leader, Amanda, who was responsible for employee well-being and championed for the app, started to feel uneasy. No one seemed to be using or talking about this app anymore.

(continued)

(continued)

When Amanda finally managed to get some usage data from the vendor, her suspicions were confirmed—adoption was terribly low. Less than 6% of the employees had even activated their account. Of those who did sign up, most stopped using it within a week.

Amanda felt disappointed and embarrassed. She had stuck her neck out to get budget approved for this app that would improve the mental health and energy levels of employees across the organization. But the data showed almost no one was actually using it. It was unclear what value users got out of it, but given such low usage, it wouldn't have mattered if the handful of users sang praises.

When it came time to renew the contract, Amanda made the difficult but necessary call to not renew. As much as she believed in the importance of offering well-being support, this solution did not work.

Making data-driven decisions is crucial, even when it means admitting something didn't go as planned.

Amanda asked the analytics team to run surveys and focus groups to better understand what employees needed for health and well-being support. As it turns out, you can't force-feed employees resources, even good ones—the key is asking, listening, and iterating based on their lived experiences.

Case Studies: Data-informed DEI and Well-being Programs

For years, I have had the privilege of witnessing the dedication and passion of several trailblazers, individuals who have integrated DEI and employee well-being principles into their work. My goal in curating these case studies is not to provide a collection of best practices or a checklist of initiatives to replicate. Instead, I hope to inspire you with real examples and show you the transformative power of data and AI.

In the following interviews, you'll gain invaluable insights from industry leaders who have successfully leveraged data and AI to drive transformative DEI and well-being initiatives within their organizations. You'll see a spectrum of experiences, ranging from people analytics leaders, chief diversity officers, well-being executives, ERG leaders, to consultants. Each story offers thought-provoking insights that are practical, whether you're a seasoned leader or just embarking on your journey.

You'll be exposed to cutting-edge techniques and innovative approaches, as well as surprisingly simple changes that made a huge impact. It's crucial to understand that AI and data are not ends in themselves; they are tools that must be used responsibly, with the ultimate goal of creating inclusive, supportive, and workplace cultures that every individual is empowered to thrive.

Dawn Klinghoffer, Vice President of HR Business Insights, Microsoft

As vice president of Microsoft's HR Business Insights, Dawn is responsible for advanced people analytics and research for all of the company's business units across the globe. This centralized team includes employee listening systems, analytics, and reporting support for such HR programs as global diversity and inclusion, global HR services, talent management, and learning and development.

I've had the pleasure of knowing Dawn for several years after speaking on the same panel a few years ago. My conversation with Dawn was enlightening as usual. The top themes are the following: **thriving and work/life balance are not the same; well-being is the pre-curser to feeling energized; the trio of people analytics, well-being, and benefits is powerful; and DEI team is key to success.**

(continued)

(continued)

Rather than employee engagement, Microsoft shifted to measure employee thriving in the middle of the pandemic as new norms emerged. **Thriving** is defined as **being energized and empowered to do meaningful work.** For Microsoft, well-being is the "energized" part of thriving. "If you are not well, you won't feel energized. It's a close proxy," said Dawn.

The research at Microsoft found that employees who are thriving are likely to have the highest scores on the indicators of high performance, such as productivity, effort, and impact.[4] Additionally, employees who say they feel energized are 44% more likely to say they feel proud of their work, and 22% more likely to say they take the initiative to be productive and put discretionary effort into their work.

The latest available data comes from the 2023 Microsoft Diversity & Inclusion Report[5] and shows the global score of 76 was made up of an average of energized (72), empowered (77), and meaningful work (80). The report compares this **thriving** score across gender and race groups to help identify any areas that require additional support and attention.

Microsoft surveys employees about "Feeling Energized" and tests the hypothesis: does **thriving** mean employees have work-life balance? The analysis shows that career is a bigger driver for thriving than work-life balance.

It may seem counterintuitive on the surface that work-life balance doesn't overlap with thriving, but Dawn explains there is a timing aspect to consider: "If you are working on a critical project with large impact and a tight deadline, you may be thriving during this period of time, but the long hours are not sustainable for years."

We ended our conversation on a positive note where Dawn confirms what I've heard in other leading organizations—the people analytics, well-being, and DEI teams do collaborate closely together. The D&I annual report shows the results of collaboration across these teams.

Dr. Alexis Fink, Vice President of People Analytics and Workforce Strategy at Meta, Former GM of Talent Management at Intel

Alexis shared one of the most fascinating examples of data analytics in DEI. She tested the hypothesis that certain experiences are the key to unlocking a new level of career success. By using longitudinal data, she was able to identify the point of divergence by comparing individuals who end up in much higher positions than others who seemed equally promising earlier in their careers. It became apparent that employees who passed through certain leaders, or "**sponsorship superheroes,**" had certain accelerator roles, or made unexpected career moves ended up progressing much farther in their careers. "Chief of staff roles are great accelerator roles, for instance. You get into rooms you'd not otherwise be in. You get to build relationships and really develop strategic acumen." said Alexis.

One area Alexis is excited about is what AI is doing for neurodiverse employees. For instance, the VR (virtual reality) headsets piloted at Meta allow employees to have a visually less distractive workspace and collaborate more effortlessly. She tested out herself too. "The environment is really immersive – it really feels like your colleagues are right there." There are lots of opportunities to level the playing field, especially with employees who have different needs.

As an I/O psychologist, Alexis is a leading expert on surveys. I asked her for recommendations on when to use quantitative versus quantitative data in understanding sensitive issues such as DEI in the workplace. She suggests combining qualitative and quantitative data for the win. "There is no replacement for qualitative when it comes to smaller samples, especially when you need to understand personal and sensitive context," said Alexis.

(continued)

(continued)

She offers this rule of thumb of using data to dig into issues: Quantitative data helps you understand "WHERE to dig," and qualitative research helps you uncover nuances in meaning.

For example, "Is there a segment that has lower engagement" is a great fit for quantitative data. However, quantitative is not as useful in certain situations. Consider conjoint analysis or trade-off analysis in well-being or benefits space. "I really value a private office and would trade X compensation for that." Think about the part-time schedule—what does it take for this to work? This type of information is difficult to gather via regular quantitative surveys.

As for the Linkage between DEI and well-being, Alexis has seen a connection between "Belonging" and "Intent to Stay" on surveys. This makes intuitive sense, since inclusion and belonging reduce the burden of covering and gives employees the energy to get more work done.

Dr. Stephanie Murphy, Founder and Principal Consultant of MCS Consulting, Founder and Executive Director of the Society for People Analytics

I've known Stephanie through people analytics events and had the joy of getting to know her as not only a fantastic analytics practitioner and educator, but also a caring leader.

Stephanie has examined carefully the impact of ERGs and her data analysis shows that those who attend ERG events have higher engagement and lower attrition. This is consistent with findings from other organizations. While it is often difficult to show causality when there are other confounding factors, it's possible to remove some of the noise by comparing the before and after rather than simply looking at participants versus nonparticipants. In the case of engagement, one might argue that highly engaged employees are more likely to join company events so the ERG events did not increase their engagement, and it's the other way around. By restricting the dataset to the same individuals and comparing their before- and after-participation data, much of the noise can be removed.

While working at a Fortune 50 technology company, Stephanie's team created an Inclusion Index that consisted of 10-questions with the goal of understanding "what inclusion means at our company," which were then reviewed by the chief diversity officer and HR leadership team.

The most unique and effective was the focus on accountability. Stephanie is proud of the role data analytics played in driving accountability at the company. The program was for three years and managers with less than five direct reports had increasing accountability each year.

- Year 1: If the inclusion score was below target, the company provided resources to these managers.
- Year 2: If the score was still below target, then a meeting with HR would be scheduled.
- Year 3: There would be disciplinary actions (e.g., bonus reduction, demotion) if the score was still below target after three years.

I know from my experience that it can be difficult to get approval from the legal team to capture data on employees' emotions, especially when there's an open-ended question that increases the risk of employees' venting about issues that are out of the company's control.

Stephanie also worked with a company to create innovative ways to pulse how employees felt about work on a regular basis through a combination of "how are you feeling" emojis and an open-ended question, "What emotions come to mind when you

(continued)

(continued)

think about work?" The three-tier red/yellow/green emoji response plus the open-ended comments gave a pulse on how employees were doing. Employees who reported positive emotions were more likely to feel included.

Stephanie also shared that surveys was just one of the tools for listening. There are other effective ways to gather data on inclusion and well-being, such as regular listening sessions. At one company she worked with, the CEO meets with different groups of employees while they share their experiences every week. This provides a direct line to leadership and an opportunity for open dialogue.

As for quantitative versus qualitative data, Stephanie uses both types of data and advises, "If you don't know where to start, go to the quantitative, and then figure out where to dive in and the 'why' using qualitative."

Overall, Stephanie's multipronged approach combines quantitative metrics, qualitative feedback, leadership involvement, and organizational network data to understand and improve the level of inclusion and well-being. By going beyond annual surveys, Stephanie's approach allows for timely action and ensures accountability longer term.

Dr. Sanja Licina, President at QuestionPro and formerly Workforce Analytics at CareerBuilder

Sanja is an I/O psychologist by training and spent years in workforce analytics at CareerBuilder before moving to the survey platform firm, QuestionPro. I've known Sanja through people analytics events and her podcast. She deeply cares about building inclusive and healthy workplaces so I was thrilled to include her in the interviews.

While QuestionPro is smaller than some other companies included in this book, their employees want similar things as those in larger companies. The surveys at QuestionPro showed that summer Fridays (half day on Fridays) had a positive impact on employee well-being.

One area where AI has improved is understanding open-ended responses. Many organizations say, "We don't know what we don't know," so the open-ended responses are helpful to understand what employees need. The survey data can show "what is true today and how can we put it into practice," said Sanja.

Surveys help us understand what is important and why. For instance, we know intuitively employees value flexible work arrangements, but do we know why they value these programs? In the employee response to the survey question of "What do you value about our culture?" flexibility often comes up in the top three.

I asked Sanja how GenAI has changed employee listening. "Companies are starting to ask more open-ended questions because of the enhanced capability to understand them," said Sanja. While GenAI can't replace researchers reading and reviewing comments today, it gets you to the story faster.

One case study from Sanja's clients is worth mentioning. A company leverages rewards and recognition data to understand changes in the levels of employee engagement. If there's a change in the recognition behavior, it would alert the manager for a conversation because these behavior changes that are tied to disengagement and potential attrition. Sanja recommends, "The most optimal setup is having both ONA [organizational network analysis] and survey data as a follow-up." We have different needs for connection, if someone interacts a lot with colleagues, are they actually satisfied with these interactions? This combination of quantitative and qualitative data is consistent with what other leading practitioners recommend.

(continued)

(continued)

For those getting started on measuring well-being and DEI, below are some sample survey questions to consider:

Well-being

- My levels of work-related stress are manageable.
- At the end of the day, I can disconnect from work and find time to rest.
- I am able to take days off when I feel the need to rest and recharge.
- My manager encourages me to take care of my emotional and physical health.
- My health and well-being matter to my manager.
- Our leaders take care of their emotional and physical health.
- Our company provides us with useful resources to maintain our well-being.
- I feel like I can achieve my objectives while still having a good balance between work and family/social life.
- I have enough energy after work to do what I want to do.
- I am satisfied with my overall well-being.

DEI

- I can be my authentic self at work; I don't have to pretend to be someone I'm not to fit in.
- I am satisfied with the amount of interaction I have with colleagues that have different backgrounds than mine.
- I am comfortable proactively reaching out to my colleagues regardless of their title or position.
- I feel like I have similar advancement opportunities to other colleagues in the organization.
- I feel that my opinions and ideas are valued and considered in decision-making.
- During meetings, I feel comfortable speaking up and providing my perspective.

- My manager makes a genuine effort to create an inclusive team environment.
- I am satisfied with how frequently our company discusses the importance of diversity.
- Our company does a good job of creating an inclusive culture.
- Our company culture makes me feel like I belong here.

Chris Cummings, Founder and CEO of Well-being at Work

Well-being at Work was started by Chris Cummings, who was inspired by his partner's mental health condition to make a positive impact on well-being in the workplace and drive positive change. I've known Chris for a few years through the well-being events he hosts and have continued to be inspired by his work on workplace well-being.

"Everyone was touched by the pandemic, which increased awareness of mental health," said Chris. One area AI has made a huge impact is the accessibility of insights. AI and GenAI advancements take away manual tasks and made data-informed insights more accessible to leaders.

When I asked Chris about the community he is building on well-being through events, he said, "Compassion has become very important since COVID." The demand for this work has increased across the globe. Cultural differences may be one but an even larger difference in how health systems work across the globe. Stigma around mental healthcare is still present. Some industries have high expectations for being on all the time and the stigma may be tougher to overcome. Culturally in parts of Asia, mental health is not as openly discussed.

"I think we need to change the conversation around well-being to be focused on performance for the business so we can

(continued)

(continued)

engage senior leaders, rather than talking about well-being as a fluffy concept," said Chris.

We discussed what holds organizations back from making progress in employee well-being. Chris responded, "It is two-fold: (1) the language we use hasn't been what the C-suite needs to hear; (2) not measuring or measuring but not connecting well-being metrics to business outcomes the C-suite cares about." I couldn't have said it better myself. This is consistent with what I've seen in leading organizations.

How has data and AI helped? AI advancement has enabled companies to bring a large amount of data together that previously would have been extremely time-consuming. It has also enabled better measures of well-being and DEI. Many organizations also use data to show how effective well-being programs have been. One of the most effective ways to show is via absenteeism and linking with performance.

Chris said the problems we can answer are now more business-focused. For example, where should we focus in the organization? Also, predictive analytics around signals for burnout and lack of belonging can give leaders a heads-up.

I asked Chris the tough question, "Whose responsibility is it to improve employee well-being?" and he said it's everyone's responsibility. Leaders set the amount of work team members have to do and can directly impact burnout in either direction. Individuals also play their part in being self-aware and realizing what is needed for them to thrive.

I also appreciated Chris sharing his personal experience during our conversation about covering. The connection between DEI and well-being is very strong. "When I hid my sexuality earlier in my career, I wasn't performing my best and my mental health was not as good because I was hiding part of myself." We need workplaces that allow people to be themselves. Covering is detrimental to our well-being.

Shujaat Ahmad, AI & Future of Work + People Analytics Pioneer, Former ERG Leader at LinkedIn

I was intrigued by Shujaat Ahmad's work because he is one of the few people analytics leaders who has a strong focus on DEIB (as he calls it diversity, equity, inclusion, and belonging) and well-being. He shared with me in the interview that DEIB was his "why" for joining people analytics at LinkedIn as one of the original team members. While DEIB analytics wasn't mature enough to be a standalone role at the time, he knew that he could make an impact in this area with his strategy and data analytics expertise.

Shujaat built a workforce representation mix model with inflow and outflow with scenario planning capability. The model brought insights on what it'll take to move the needle on diversity. However, that was just one piece of the puzzle. He combined that with qualitative insights from the grassroot level through his extracurricular work with employee communities (e.g., employee resource groups) to make sense of what the quantitative data was saying.

"Diversity is a small data problem; we make the mistake of only applying a big data lens to it," said Shujaat. "The magic is in combining both. It leads to actionable insights". Shujaat added that "Analytics teams don't often go beyond just the data, and miss out on building perspectives that are relevant to the context of the organization and people on the ground. They end up doing analytics for the sake of analytics, and not to solve the business problem."

The insights-focused approach was helpful to challenge the convention that if 95% say a solution is working, then it must be working for the organization, as some underserved groups make up less than 5% of the employee population. That 5% may have some of your top performing and most critical talent in critical roles but you would never know.

(continued)

(continued)

Shujaat also led the Embrace ERG as their Global co-chair at LinkedIn. His leadership work was awarded by the CEO two years in a row during the difficult time of the COVID-19 pandemic lockdown and post George Floyd civic unrest including employee activism within companies. The ERG focused on education to help people embrace differences across different cultures and layers of identities. He led the work on difficult topics on identity in a unique way focused on education through celebrations of arts, food, and sports to bring harmony and allyship for individuals from all backgrounds, cultures, and nationalities. Originally there was a strong focus on ex-pats in EMEA but quickly expanded into focusing on intersectionality in general.

In Shujaat's portfolio of work as a AI & Future Work advisor, DEIB culture change to drive outcomes is a key element of his design. He has pioneered bringing data to what conventional approaches deem difficult to measure or extremely difficult to get legal approval. For instance, at his clients, DEIB teams and ERGs have wanted to get insights on nationalities so they can design cultural programming. Shujaat's first principles approach has been that our objective is to get V1 of cultural programming going that drives belonging. To get there, we just need directionally correct insights to get some level of programming going. We don't need perfect data. We need enough to build moments of belonging around nationalities and more people will step up as volunteers without going through the hassle of capturing nationality data. This has included creative methods like putting up a map in offices with pins for employees to anonymously mark "Where is home for You?". This is then combined with employee surveys asking questions like "What cultural celebration would drive a sense of belonging for you". Combining the two sources of insights has given enough insights for DEIB teams to build their cultural programming while abiding with data privacy.

There's a strong focus on well-being and burnout at LinkedIn during the pandemic.

Similarly, there continues to be a strong focus on well-being and burnout since the pandemic. With employee sentiment on their experience and how work is organized, blended with team collaboration patterns and behaviors from network analysis, Shujaat has linked how employees were doing and their sense of belonging with their individual and team work behaviors. He has helped answer for leaders who wanted to know, "At what point do employees get into burnout zones? And how that is being fueled by how I am running my team?"

Of course, leaders want to know how productivity is impacted when employees are not feeling included. Unlike other metrics, productivity is one where there isn't a standard definition. Shujaat shared creative ways to measure productivity at LinkedIn. First, they ask the employees and managers, "What is productivity?" Then they use the dimensions to create survey questions such as "I am able to get work done," "I am able to create new ideas," "I am able to get mentorship," etc. These self-rated answers become nuanced measures of productivity measures that leaders and employees resonate with as they are relevant to the context of their business, instead of the ambiguous single item measures to suit a specific leader's narrative.

During the pandemic and coming out of the pandemic, leaders have been interested in how remote or hybrid work was impacting employees' productivity. In Shujaat's portfolio of clients, he used data integrated across employee surveys, workforce location and office presence data, active ONA, passive ONA, and focus groups. His analysis has shown no negative impact of distributed work on productivity overall. However, the data have shown there are a lot of nuances. For instance, employees often report high productivity while working remotely, but they also have a low level of connection because of the lack of interactions. Connection in general has been positively correlated with productivity, though of course there is variation across individuals on how much connection is optimal. More connection also isn't

(continued)

(continued)

better; there are diminishing returns. The key is intentional and meaningful connections.

Another topic we discussed in our conversation was "covering." Shujaat said that covering was difficult to measure directly, but you can get signals for covering like a survey question around "comfort in speaking up" and "trusting how the survey will be used."

Shujaat shared some innovative ways to measure the illusive concept of culture and quantifying cultural change. These include both analyzing town hall transcripts and asking employees to describe culture on surveys. In the world of LLMs (Gen AI) now, these can be done fast and easily now.

If leaders say certain values are key to our culture, do leaders reflect that in their public and private communications? Shujaat has helped teams leverage natural language processing (NLP) on company communication transcripts such as townhalls that most companies do regularly. In some cases, there was a gap between what the leaders said were the values and what ended up in their town hall messages to employees. This has helped partnering employee communications to drive culture change through leadership communications as a vessel for change. Similarly, employees should be able to tell leaders what their culture is. He has been creative in asking employees to describe culture in a few adjectives. In some cases, the results have been positively surprising for some companies. Compassion, diversity, inclusion, and belonging have come up as top descriptions which has helped business and HR leadership teams know efforts have successfully reached employees, and DEIB wasn't just an empty word on the wall.

One of the most interesting findings is that there is a strong connection between successful remote or hybrid work and inclusion. Having a sense of inclusion is what makes remote work successful. Pre-pandemic, companies that were remote were successful because the norms were set up for equality and equity. The data helps inform remote work did work and what makes the setup successful within the company. It also highlights the importance of leaders' and managers' ability to operate in a remote setting. I've been pondering about this last point since our conversation. I hope organizations start to pay closer attention to managers' leadership skills as we navigate through return-to-office debates.

César A. Lostaunau, HR director and ERG leader, Morningstar, Anywhere Real Estate, and Allstate Insurance

César has had a nontraditional career path that took him from IT to HR. While at Allstate, he led the PLAN (Professional Latino Allstate Network) ERG. One of the struggles the business had was building a diverse talent pipeline. César knew it was critical to show impact of the ERG and he asked to create a separate referral link so Allstate could start tracking how many referrals came from ERG members.

On top of helping with the talent pipeline through referrals, PLAN also helped referrals with interview readiness and organizational insights to elevate the candidate's confidence and chances for success. Specifically, César described the interview prep as an equity play, where they intentionally connect candidates with leaders and facilitate the networking. Separately, the talent acquisition team didn't always have the Spanish skills to assess candidates in markets where Spanish is a required skill, so PLAN leaders and members jumped in and helped assess candidates. Eventually this effort resulted in the implementation of a language assessment software for more efficient screening.

Transparency was not just a buzzword at Allstate. As an ERG leader, César had visibility to employee survey analysis comparing how ERG members compare with other employees, including

(continued)

(continued)

other ERGs. The engagement survey data showed ERG members are the most engaged and satisfied. In my conversations, this level of transparency is rare because the typical practice is not sharing employee data with ERG leaders. An additional and realistic challenge is that ERG participation is not often a data field in the HR system, so many employee surveys do not have this dimension for slicing and dicing.

We discussed the role of ERG in developing talent while the company has a learning and development (L&D) team. Cesar focused on the development that would be high-impact and not offered by the L&D team. He fought for the board members of the ERG to get coaching individually from a multicultural coach. This served both as a "thank you" for ERG board members volunteering their time and a tool to demystify coaching.

The most impressive data work I've seen is the ERG Dashboard César built. Knowing it is not enough to see employee survey data for ERG members once a year, he created a dashboard with real-time data showing how ERG membership was correlated with performance, promotions, and retention. For now, only HR has access to this dashboard, but I can see the power longer term and applaud César for bringing real-time data to the business.

Carlo Dela Fuente, Chief of Staff, Director of Business Operations and Connected Asian Affinity Network Leader at Cisco

Several years ago, Carlo noticed the need for leadership training for employees in the ERG Connected Asian American Network (CAAN). He explored several different leadership development offerings from major external organizations and finally settled on the nonprofit Leadership Education for Asian Pacifics (LEAP) to provide training and turned it into a program. Instead of a one and done training, he approached development as an ongoing cohort program, building tight knit small groups that supported one another and benefited from sustained executive coaching engagements well beyond the "in class" experience to maximize ROI and provide the ability to measure progress. The leadership development program was designed for people who wanted to be leaders or promoted to the next level. Thus far 150+ have gone through the program.

Founded in 1982, LEAP is a national, nonprofit organization, with a mission to achieve full participation and equality for Asian and Pacific Islanders (APIs) through leadership, empowerment, and policy. LEAP offers programs aiming to increase the success of their API high potential talent to lead effectively and advance in their careers.

After five years of collaboration, LEAP is now an official partner for a leadership development program portfolio within Cisco. Rarely do ERG-led programs become corporate-wide programs; it was clear that Carlo demonstrated the impact of the LEAP partnership.

In addition to regular NPS on surveys, "Do you feel more ready for promotion?" is asked in the survey and received very positive responses from program participants. Carlo didn't stop there. He followed up with the program participants and found that 30% to 40% of participants got promoted after the program.

Under Carlo's leadership, CAAN is not only thriving but also charitable. CAAN is the most generous ERG in Cisco with half a million dollars donated toward social justice. The recipe for excellence is clear. The leaders for successful ERGs run it like a business.

One of the boldest programs I've heard in my interviews is the multiplier effect at Cisco. The multiplier effect is built on the idea of sponsorship, which is more than mentoring. The leaders make a personal commitment to be an advocate for a diverse candidate. It is asking leaders to step out of their comfort zone and

(continued)

(continued)

be accountable for the success of someone different from them in race, culture, ability, gender, generation, ethnicity, or orientation. One hundred percent of Cisco leaders at or above vice president level have pledged as of 2023.

Another progressive change in Cisco's data approach is the self-ID initiative for Asian employees. Since Asians are not homogenous, it was important to have the space to share (i.e., Hmong, Filipinos). Within the Asian community, East and South Asian employees may have different needs. When employees opt to participate in self-ID, the data can help create a more inclusive experience for employees, informing decisions on resourcing and support.

Tashi Theisman, VP of Global Benefits

I've had the joy of working with Tashi while she was leading global benefits at PayPal. She is the most data-driven leader in this space I've seen, and I was so happy to be able to highlight her work in this book.

She is a continuous learner at heart and shares that many research studies use employee engagement as a proxy for workplace well-being, which is correlated with business outcomes like turnover and absenteeism. She has been successful in getting well-being programs funded because she speaks the language business leaders care about. As an example, she advocates collecting better data on employee well-being by showing hard numbers on healthcare costs and absenteeism impact from improving well-being.

When she led global benefits at another technology firm, the company created a global well-being dashboard. In the United States, the company measured health risks (1–5), and each additional health risk is equated to increased specific dollar of claims costs. It was clear how much it would save for employees to move down the risks spectrum. It not only saved on health claims, it also helped improve several other measures such as health outcomes, productivity, and the culture of well-being (based on a 10-question survey for employees).

We discussed the power and limitations of AI in employee well-being. One thing she recommends to other leaders considering AI pilots is to make sure "your house is clean." If a company wants to use chatbots to answer employee questions, for instance, the chatbot may not know whether the policy is up-to-date, and this can result in giving out the wrong information. For companies with footprints in 50+ countries, they can easily have more than 50 country-specific policies. If there have been updates to these documents, it's critical to remove the old policies from the system so the chatbot doesn't read the wrong policy.

Tashi's superpower is her focus on value creation from well-being programs. For year, she has led the buildout of holistic programs for health and well-being. It was data-driven as the CEO demanded to see ROI on these programs. She continued to show to each CEO when she proposes a new program, "This will pay for itself."

We talked about how well-being and inclusion and diversity teams partner across her companies. "The connection with those supporting underserved communities is strong," she said. In Tashi's experience, she has partnered with chief diversity officers and ERGs: For instance, her department implemented health programs for Black and Latino communities with respect to medical coverage because of different social determinants of health. ERGs help ensure different groups can get the help they need. ERGs also help with listening efforts to get feedback. She has partnered with women's ERG and women in tech groups across different companies. Some of the most effective programs included specific coaching for women and adding benefits for care takers.

Cindi Howson, Chief Data Strategy Officer, ThoughtSpot

Cindi hosted me on her Data Chief podcast a few years ago, and I've had the pleasure of meeting her at various data conferences since then. Through our informal chats, I've come to learn that Cindi has a strong passion for DEI and advocating for women in data.

For years, we have all heard that tech has a DEI problem. But without data it is impossible to know where the problem is and how to solve it. When Cindi first joined ThoughtSpot, there was very little visibility to employee data when it comes to demographic backgrounds. As a data company, Cindi practiced what she preached and made the diversity representation data available to all employees at ThoughtSpot. Privacy is protected, of course, so there is no drill downs to see names of individuals who self-identify as a particular demographic.

Cindi believes DEI has to be owned by everyone, not just HR or people ops. To achieve this, there has to be transparency. "We have to tell people where they stand," she says. This turned into a SpotApp that the customers of ThoughtSpot can directly leverage by connecting to their HR data.

For the measures of inclusion, Thoughtspot uses CultureAmp and hired an external firm to conduct conversations around the sense of inclusion. When we analyzed the employee NPS score, we know that inclusion and workload management influence it most.

Transparency and privacy are important. "You have to have multiple forms of trusted communication in a company. If someone is having a bad day, week, or month, they may not want everyone to know. Surveys, even if confidential, are only one of the mechanisms. Sometimes you need to create a safe space to have real conversations instead," she said. Qualitative data gathering "tell me what you are working on that you are excited about or that you are not."

Bias in AI is a concern, and diversity is the problem. For example, type in "show me an example of a beautiful person" and AI will give you the stereotypes. It is estimated that there are only 30% of women in AI globally. How can we increase this?

Dan Riley, Cofounder of RADICL

Dan is an expert on employee experience and works with leaders and organizations around the world helping them to meet the moment and mobilize for the future. Dan recently cofounded RADICL after cofounding Modern Survey in 1999 and selling it to Aon in 2016.

Dan's research shows that people with great employee experience have twice the level of productivity, five times the rate of retention, and four times the rate of engagement versus people with a toxic or pressure-cooker experience.

We also discussed the topic of employee well-being, and Dan's data analysis across clients shows several drivers of well-being:

- **Work-life Balance:** Flexible hours, remote work, and adequate time off
- **Mental Health Support:** Access to counseling, stress management, and mental health days
- **Physical Health:** Health benefits, safety, and ergonomic support
- **Meaningful Work:** Job autonomy, purpose, and alignment with personal values
- **Recognition:** Regular feedback, fair compensation, and appreciation
- **Supportive Leadership:** Trust, open communication, and empathy from management
- **Career Development:** Opportunities for growth, learning, and clear career pathways

(continued)

(continued)

- **Inclusion:** Diverse, inclusive culture and a sense of belonging
- **Positive Work Environment:** Strong relationships and positive workplace culture
- **Financial Wellness:** Fair pay, financial security programs, and support for financial literacy

The connection of career development and well-being echoes what other research has found, and so "inclusion" is a top driver for well-being.

I asked Dan to share the top reasons for employees leaving the company, from both quantitative and qualitative data. Is it true that money doesn't matter as much? We have been hearing about purpose being important, but is that more important than salary? Following are the top reasons employees have shared.

- **Lack of Career Growth:** Employees feel stuck with no clear path for advancement, skill development, or professional opportunities, prompting them to seek roles that offer growth potential.
- **Uncompetitive Pay** (removing the sharp edges): When employees believe their compensation isn't keeping up with market rates or their contributions, they are more likely to look for better-paying opportunities elsewhere.
- **Poor Work-life Balance:** Excessive workloads, rigid schedules, and little flexibility create burnout, leading employees to seek jobs that offer more balance and respect for personal time.
- **Toxic Workplace Culture:** Negative work environments, work politics, or a *lack of support and collaboration/connection drive people away* from toxic workspaces in search of healthier, more positive environments.

- **Poor Management:** Ineffective, unsupportive, or micro-managing leaders cause frustration, erode trust, and leave employees feeling unvalued, pushing them to find companies with better leadership.

I closed the interview chatting with Dan about focus groups. It's an area where many organizations have not had the expertise and might not know where to start. The key is to keep them open-ended and easy to answer. It's important to get the dialogue going. His favorite questions are these fill in the blank questions:

- I love it when....
- I don't like it when....
- I wish we could...

Dan recommends these three focus group questions to understand employee experience for organizations that want to get started:

- What motivates you to come to work each day, and what would make it even better?

  This helps uncover what employees value most about their work and environment while highlighting areas for improvement in motivation and engagement.
- How supported do you feel in balancing your professional and personal life, and what changes would enhance that balance?"

  This question reveals insights into the company's work-life balance policies and how well they align with employee needs, providing a window into the company's culture around flexibility and support.
- If you could change one thing about how we work or communicate as a team, what would it be?

  This encourages honest feedback on team dynamics, communication, and collaboration, helping to identify underlying issues within the company's culture and areas to improve teamwork.

Lani Hall, Global Diversity and Inclusion Leader, J.M. Huber Corporation, GE Energy, and GE Aviation

I've known Lani for almost 10 years and worked with her closely at GE Aviation when I led People Analytics at the company. She is one of the most data-savvy and business-focused leaders I've met. It was such a joy to interview her for this book.

I asked her about the biggest impact data analytics has made during her career, and she described in detail how she quantified the benefits of flexibility at GE in the early 2000s. This was 20 years before COVID, and most assumed that employees who worked from home were less productive.

Here's the problem. The office was getting crowded and running out of space for every employee. When Lani looked at the cost, the office space was 10 times more costly than providing remote work setup to employees on a per person basis. To ensure incentives were aligned, managers who agreed to allowing employees to work remotely got the cost savings back in their budget. This created traction for reluctant managers to give remote work a try in the early 2000s.

Still, not every manager was convinced the cost savings would be worth the productivity loss. The perception was that remote workers would not be as productive. Lani brought data analytics into the conversation. She compared the employee performance ratings before and after they went remote. To many leaders' surprise, employees had higher performance ratings after going remote on average. When asked in a follow-up conversation, these employees said they were more productive at home due to less interruptions compared to being in the office.

That wasn't all. There were also benefits when it comes to retention. Managers thought "out of sight, out of mind" so employees who weren't in the office must be more likely to quit. The data showed retention was two times higher for those who were working remotely.

I smiled at these myth-busting data analytics in my conversation with Lani. This is the benefit of thinking like a scientist in the corporate world. Being open-minded to what the data might say instead of assuming is what it takes for organizations to become truly data-driven.

An aspect that improved employee well-being is providing transparency around promotability. Many top talent feel anxious because they never knew they were top talent and had no idea where they stood in the organization. Lani was influential in creating transparency around the potential of employees. I was reminded that I didn't always know I was in a high potential program until I explicitly asked.

More recently, Lani also introduced psychological safety as one of the competencies for every career level in her organization. Employees rate themselves, and managers also provide their assessment on performance evaluations. While the company provided psychological safety training, Lani wanted to make sure the competency of employees did increase after the trainings. I admire the high level of accountability she brings to every company, and I also realize none of this would have been possible without a clear data analytics strategy.

I've seen many organizations design and implement DEI programs without a clear business outcome in mind, including training programs, and became disappointed at how the programs turned out. One unique aspect that stands out from Lani's deep expertise and experience is that she designs DEI programs based on the outcome and metrics the business wants to improve. This approach brings a level of thoughtfulness that ensures a win-win for the company and its employees.

These interviews from across industries help paint a picture of what successful organizations have done to create a thriving workplace. The key takeaways are as follows:

- Leaders of successful DEI and well-being programs treat them as strategic business initiatives and are experts at connecting the efforts to financial metrics to gain C-suite attention.
- The recent accessibility of GenAI has transformed data analysis in DEI and well-being, enabling companies to process large amounts of data more efficiently and ask more open-ended questions to employees, leading to enhanced measures and insights of well-being and DEI.
- AI is increasingly integrated into employee well-being initiatives. For example, AI-powered chatbots are being used to answer employee questions about benefits and well-being programs, improving accessibility and efficiency.
- AI technologies are improving the work lives of neurodivergent employees, offering tools that enhance their productivity and well-being, including converting speech-to-text or text-to-speech and using sensory-friendly technology for those with sensory sensitivities and communication difficulties.
- Advanced analytics, including AI-powered techniques like NLP and ONA, have provided nuanced insights into employee collaboration and communications.
- Qualitative data are crucial for understanding low N-size situations and sensitive contexts, complementing quantitative data in guiding decision-making and strategy.
- Transparency in career growth and creating psychologically safe environments are crucial for employee well-being, especially for underrepresented groups, with ERGs playing a vital role in improving career outcomes and providing feedback.
- While AI offers powerful capabilities, leaders must ensure that underlying data and policies are up-to-date when implementing AI solutions to avoid misinformation. Pilot within a small area, proper testing process, and data governance are the keys to successful implementation.

- Leading organizations have a strong connection between DEI and well-being in the workplace, with leaders adopting a holistic approach and collaborating across people analytics, DEI, and well-being teams.
- Collaboration with legal and privacy teams is vital when collecting new data points, requiring early involvement and effective storytelling to highlight the benefits of additional data collection.

As we continue into the next part of this book, we will shift our focus toward the future of work. We will discuss both AI's impact on DEI and well-being, and address how to stay human-centered in the age of AI.

Notes

1. Freifeld, L. (2023). *Training APEX awards best practice: #LearnLikeAnOwner at Kraft Heinz.* Training. Available at: https://trainingmag.com/training-apex-awards-best-practice-learnlikeanowner-at-kraft-heinz/

2. Catalino, N., Gardner, N., Goldstein, D., and Wong, J. (2022). *Effective employee resource groups are key to inclusion at work. Here's how to get them right.* McKinsey. Available at: https://www.mckinsey.com/capabilities/people-and-organizational-performance/our-insights/effective-employee-resource-groups-are-key-to-inclusion-at-work-heres-how-to-get-them-right

3. Durruthy, R. (2020). *Employee resource groups help strengthen connection in times of uncertainty.* Fast Company. Available at: https://www.fastcompany.com/90511029/employee-resource-groups-help-strengthen-connection-in-times-of-uncertainty [Accessed 3 Nov. 2024].

4. Microsoft. (2023). *There are no shortcuts to high performance.* Available at: https://www.microsoft.com/en-us/worklab/there-are-no-shortcuts-to-high-performance

5. Microsoft. (2024). *Diversity & inclusion report.* Available at: https://www.microsoft.com/en-us/diversity/inside-microsoft/annual-report

Chapter 5

The Impact of AI on DEI and Well-being

As AI becomes ever more integrated into our work lives, it brings both benefits and risks when it comes to progress in DEI and well-being. In this chapter, we will explore how AI can serve as a powerful catalyst for creating a thriving workplace, while also addressing the potential risks.

The Double-edge Sword: AI's Potential and Risks to Advancing DEI

There is tremendous potential for AI to advance an organization's progress on DEI, including bias reduction, accessibility enhancement, and career development personalization.

Reduce or Identify Bias and Data-informed Hiring

I still remember the shock I felt when I first read "Are Emily and Greg More Employable Than Lakisha and Jamal? A Field Experiment on Labor Market Discrimination" by Bertrand and Mullainathan[1] in graduate school. It was published in the top economic journal *American Economic Review*. The researchers randomly assigned Black- or White-sounding names to resumes in the experiment and found that White names receive 50% more callbacks for interviews. This racial gap was uniform across occupation, industry, and even employer size.

More recent research has shown that candidates of color are choosing to Whiten their resumes to boost their chances at getting selected for an interview. Does it work? It appears so. In one study, the researchers created resumes for Black and Asian applicants and sent them out for 1,600 entry-level jobs posted on job search websites in 16 metropolitan sections of the United States. Some of the resumes included information that clearly pointed out the applicants' race/ethnicity status as a minority, while others were Whitened, or scrubbed of racial clues. The researchers then created email accounts and phone numbers for the applicants and observed how many were invited for interviews.

In fact, companies are more than twice as likely to call applicants who are non-White for interviews if they submit Whitened resumes than candidates who reveal their race—and this discriminatory practice is just as strong for businesses that claim to value diversity as those that don't.

Katherine A. DeCelles, the James M. Collins Visiting Associate Professor of Business Administration at Harvard Business School, says "Discrimination still exists in the workplace.... Organizations now have an opportunity to recognize this issue as a pinch point, so they can do something about it."

Employer callbacks for resumes that were Whitened fared much better in the application pile than those that included ethnic information, even though the qualifications listed were identical. Twenty-five percent of Black candidates received callbacks from their Whitened resumes, while only 10% got calls when they left ethnic details intact. Among Asians, 21% got calls if they used Whitened resumes, whereas only 11.5% heard back if they sent resumes with racial references.

The most surprising finding is that pro-diversity employers aren't better. What's worse for minority applicants: When an employer says it values diversity in its job posting by including words like "equal opportunity employer" or "minorities are strongly encouraged to apply," many minority applicants get the false impression that it's safe to reveal their race on their resumes—only to be rejected later.

In one study to test whether minorities Whiten less often when they apply for jobs with employers that seem diversity-friendly, the researchers asked some participants to craft resumes for jobs that included pro-diversity statements and others to write resumes for jobs that didn't mention diversity.

They found minorities were half as likely to Whiten their resumes when applying for jobs with employers who said they care about diversity. But these applicants who let their guard down about their race ended up inadvertently hurting their chances of being considered: employers claiming to be pro-diversity discriminated against resumes with racial references just as much as employers who didn't mention diversity at all in their job ads.[2]

Is it possible for AI technology to reduce the need for candidates of color to Whiten their resume? Would combining technology and keeping humans in the loop make the hiring process more efficient and fair?

Imagine hiring based on whether the candidate can do the job based on their skills rather than where someone went to school or where they worked before. The technology for skills matching exists and for the longest time part of the problem was the resume itself. There has been inequality in the resume itself. Those who had access to professional resume writers could provide a resume that gets them an interview at a higher rate than those who couldn't. GenAI has enabled lots of job seekers who couldn't afford resume coaches or who aren't native speakers to update their resume for the job they are applying to.

Imagine the hiring success criteria is based on analysis of previous candidates and hires, where the experiences and skills that make someone successful in that particular role is given more weight in the new search process. For example, if account managers from other mid-size companies in healthcare with great negotiation skills make the best account managers in your organizations.

In an ideal world, this is not done in silos in disconnected ways where the analytics team conducts the study and offers the recommendations to hiring managers, but automated in the systems where each open role has these "success criteria" based on analysis of the organization's data.

Promotions is another area where traditionally DEI efforts have tried to improve. AI could call out negative patterns impacting some groups, leading to fairer performance evaluations and promotions. Companies like Textio provide text analytics technology that highlights problematic languages in talent practices such as performance reviews. With the advancement in GenAI, it is easier than ever to design processes where fairness is at the center.

Enable Accessibility for Neurodivergent and Disabled Employees

Steve Jobs, the founder and pioneer design thinker, had dyslexia. Emma Watson, famously known for her role as Hermione Granger from the Harry Potter series, has attention-deficit/hyperactivity disorder (ADHD). There are many more innovators and disruptors out there who are different.

Neurodiverse individuals, including those with autism, learning disabilities, and ADHD, bring a wealth of creative problem-solving skills, attention to detail, and innovative thinking to the table.

While the media sometimes paints neurodiverse individuals as a single group, there are several different types of neurodiversity:

- **Autism Spectrum Disorder (ASD):** A neurological and developmental disorder that affects social interaction, communication, learning, and behavior
- **Learning Disabilities:**
  - **Dyslexia:** Difficulty with reading and language processing
  - **Dyscalculia:** Difficulty with numbers and math concepts
  - **Dyspraxia:** Difficulty with coordination and motor skills
  - **Dysgraphia:** Difficulty with writing and fine motor skills
- **Attention-Deficit/Hyperactivity Disorder (ADHD):** A persistent pattern of inattention and/or hyperactivity-impulsivity that can impact daily functioning and development

Autistic individuals are usually hyper-focused, which can prevent them from grasping other relevant information during an interaction. On the other hand, ADHD individuals lose focus quickly as their attention span is limited. How can AI help? AI could identify this and automate the workflow to allow them to focus on the critical tasks. It could mean less distractions and more direction for ADHD individuals. While not every organization can provide "sensory rooms," virtual reality headsets can simulate the same environment for those with ADHD to have a less distracting workspace.

Additionally, AI could make a workplace more accessible for people with disabilities, such as through speech recognition systems. By acknowledging and accommodating these differences, we can tap into this underutilized talent pool and reap the benefits for our organizations.

Nudges to Correct Noninclusive Behaviors in Real Time

"Did you mean to also invite Amy to this meeting?" Imagine if your calendar asks you a question when you've invited everyone on your team except Amy to a meeting. It's for a meeting about a project Amy isn't on, and you didn't think Amy would join the meeting. But now you think to yourself, "Perhaps I should give Amy the choice rather than deciding for her."

Now imagine your phone reminds you as you are about to send another invite, "Your proposed meeting is taking place at 6 p.m. local time for Derek and John. Would you like to find a different time for this meeting?" Would you be more mindful of the impact you might have on the well-being and work-life balance of your colleagues?

This isn't the future.

In a 2022 article, researchers at Stanford found hundreds of firms were using AI to improve inclusion and belonging. The article opens with:

> Picture it: At 11 a.m. on a Thursday, you get a personalized Slack notification prompting you to connect with a colleague you haven't seen in a while. Then, at a midday team meeting on Zoom, you are alerted about who is speaking up less, so you can invite them to contribute. Later that day, while you are writing, an AI-powered plugin prompts you to use "chairperson" instead of "chairman." The next day, in preparation for a quarterly check-in

with a supervisee, you look at a dashboard that shares how people in your team are doing (data from pulse surveys and "listening tools" like text analysis, video, and always-on surveys suggest that your team is feeling highly connected to you and other teammates through one-on-ones, but that they may be feeling burnt out.)

Welcome to a new era of workplace digital surveillance and AI. Are you ready to belong?[3]

- Of the tools aiming to improve inclusion and belonging, 32.3% focus on data analytics. They collect and disseminate real-time information around elements of belonging via—or as alternatives to—surveys.
- Another 26.5% focus on behavior change to help advance belonging. Behavioral tools often use digital nudges, while a few send reminders and collect feedback on e-learning and development opportunities.
- And 41.2% focus on both data analytics and behavior change. They collect and analyze different data points around belonging and use insights from that data to deliver nudges, actionable strategies for improvement, or recommendations for learning and development.

Overlaying demographic data on network behaviors can identify blind spots in an organization. A 2021 *MIT Sloan Review* article finds gender and race disparities in how new hires establish their network.[4] Black women and Latino men in the sample, on average, had fewer early network ties within their functional or project groups and sustained fewer connections across functions and geographies than people in other subgroups. In contrast, Asian males made more of those connections, reaching out to key stakeholders in ways that got them drawn into work streams. "Some populations, like Black men and Asian women, were more likely than others to create cohesive internal communities with members of their subgroup. Other subgroups did not create such affinities and sometimes showed avoidance of specific subpopulations."

Perhaps more interestingly, the study also touches on promotion and retention. Among all people of color, regardless of gender, employees who enjoyed rapid promotion and those who stayed with the organization longer were, on average, more likely than others to reach out *early* to key stakeholders to understand their needs. Additionally, higher promotion and retention rates also correlated with less insular networks that allowed people to produce more creative and comprehensive solutions over time. Being sought out over time was strongly associated with faster promotion and longer tenure.

This finding has important implications for inclusion because it suggests that organizations should promote a wider breadth of connectivity rather than just vertical access to senior people in the hierarchy or connections to similar peers through employee resource groups.

Recommend Personalized Career Development

We have been talking about the "Netflix of learning" for years where you are served personalized content for training and development purposes, but how does that work to improve DEI?

We know that one of the top reasons employees leave for other companies is career development. Traditional career development programs often fall short in addressing the needs of underrepresented groups. These programs may perpetuate biases, limiting opportunities for growth and advancement, and fail to provide targeted support, leaving underrepresented groups behind. There are several areas AI-based career development can improve DEI.

AI can identify specific skills gaps and areas for improvement among underrepresented groups, enabling organizations to develop targeted training programs that address these needs. This ensures that all employees have the opportunity to acquire the skills and knowledge necessary for career advancement. Imagine if your organization uses feedback to identify managers who are less inclusive and provide daily tips and regular trainings to them.

Additionally, AI can facilitate the matching of mentors and sponsors based on shared interests, skills, and career goals. This helps create a more inclusive and supportive environment where employees can receive guidance and support from experienced leaders.

Finally, AI can analyze performance data to identify potential biases in performance evaluations and provide feedback that is objective and unbiased. This helps ensure that performance reviews are fair and equitable for all employees. Research has shown significant differences in the types of performance feedback men and women receive at work. One study revealed that women were 1.4 times as likely as men to receive critical subjective feedback.[5] Another research found that reviewers tend to prioritize niceness when reviewing women,[6] which can reinforce gender stereotypes and hold women back.

As the head of people analytics, this is one analysis my team and I would run on a regular basis to understand potential biases. The data often show differences across gender and race, though the magnitude often varies depending on the industry and function. Given the legal ramifications, I'd recommend getting approval from the legal and labor and employment teams before attempting to identify biases in the performance evaluations text and ratings data.

AI is certainly powerful in DEI, but there are abundant risks associated with AI as well.

Biases in AI Development and Deployment

The recent controversy surrounding AI-powered plagiarism detection tools highlights the urgent need to address bias in AI development. These tools, designed to identify instances of plagiarism, have been accused of unfairly targeting nonnative English speakers, highlighting a fundamental flaw: AI systems are only as good as the data they are trained on.[7]

This is not an isolated incident. AI systems used for hiring, loan approvals, and even criminal justice are susceptible to biases embedded in the data they are trained on. These biases often reflect historical inequalities, perpetuating discrimination against marginalized groups.

In the workplace, the most problematic area is the use of AI in hiring and talent management. An IBM survey from late 2023, involving more than 8,500 IT professionals worldwide, found that 42% are already using AI for screening in recruitment and HR processes, with another 40% planning to implement it.[8]

However, a growing body of evidence suggests that the reality may be more complex than initially anticipated. While many corporate leaders believed AI would eliminate hiring biases, the opposite is proving true in some cases. There's a growing concern that these AI tools may be inadvertently filtering out the most capable candidates, creating a new set of challenges for diversity and inclusion.

The investigative reporter and NYU journalism professor, Hilke Schellmann, demystifies how organizations use automation software that not only propagate bias, but fail at the thing they claim to do: find the best candidate for the job. In her book, *The Algorithm*, Schellmann asserts that the primary threat of this software isn't the replacement of human jobs by machines, but rather barring skilled individuals from securing employment.

In 2020, Anthea Mairoudhiou, a UK-based makeup artist, was instructed to reapply for her position post-furlough. Despite her skill-set scoring high, the AI tool HireVue rated her body language poorly, resulting in job loss. Following criticism, HireVue discontinued its facial analysis feature in 2021. Schellmann notes other workers have lodged complaints against similar systems, highlighting the potential for algorithmic bias to negatively impact qualified candidates.

What rights do job candidates have? The Workday lawsuit may shed some light. The Workday class action lawsuit alleges that the company's AI-powered hiring tools discriminated against a job applicant based on his race, age, and disability. The plaintiff, Mobley, claims he was rejected from more than 100 positions despite being qualified and argues that Workday should be held liable as an "employment agency" or "employer" under civil rights laws.

While Workday initially argued it was not subject to such laws, the court allowed Mobley's claims of disparate impact to proceed, finding that Workday could be liable as an "employer" due to its role in screening applicants. This ruling is significant as it could set a precedent for holding AI vendors responsible for discriminatory outcomes from their hiring tools. The Equal Employment Opportunity Commission's support for the lawsuit further emphasizes the need for scrutiny and accountability in the use of AI in hiring. The case is likely to have far-reaching consequences, potentially requiring AI vendors to ensure their tools are fair and nondiscriminatory, while also placing greater responsibility on employers to monitor and test these tools.

The bias in AI is not a technological problem; it's a *human* problem. The lack of diversity in the STEM workforce, particularly in the field of AI, is a major contributing factor.

The World Economic Forum reported women make up only less than one-third (29%) of all STEM workers.[9] The US Department of Labor Statistics showed that Black professionals account for only 9% in math and computer science. *This lack of representation means that AI systems are being developed by a narrow range of perspectives, leading to blind spots and unintended consequences.* There needs to be systematic changes to make a career in STEM more appealing to women and people of color.

The Danger of Deepfakes

Deepfakes are creating a new and alarming form of gender-based violence. This technology, which allows for the realistic manipulation of images and videos, is being weaponized against women, particularly young women, with devastating consequences.

Imagine a 16-year-old girl, facing a common adolescent conflict with classmates or going through her first breakup. The next day, she finds herself the victim of a deepfake, featuring intimate content used as revenge. This is no longer a hypothetical scenario; it's a reality for many teenage girls and women across the globe.

Deepfakes are not just a technological curiosity. They are being used for extortion, the illegal sale of explicit content, and even the manipulation of political discourse. The early days of deepfake technology saw celebrities like Scarlett Johansson and Jennifer Lawrence targeted. Now, the threat has shifted to everyday women, with potentially devastating consequences for their reputations and personal safety.

The pervasiveness of online harm is undeniable. A Centre for International Governance Innovation (CIGI) survey spanning 18 countries revealed that 60% of respondents had experienced at least 1 of the 13 forms of online abuse:

- Physically threatened online (e.g., a death threat, rape threat, threat of physical harm)
- Blackmailed online (e.g., someone threatening to post private information about them unless they did something in return, including sextortion)
- Monitored, tracked, or spied on online (e.g., by GPS location, or someone keeping track of what they say or do online)
- Someone accessing devices or social media accounts belonging to them without permission
- Called discriminatory names or derogatory cultural terms (e.g., sexist or racist names)
- Personal nude or sexual images of them shared or shown to someone else or posted online without permission (nonconsensual use of intimate images)
- Unwanted sexual images sent to them
- Having personal contact information or address posted online without permission (doxing)
- Lies posted online about them (defamation)
- Online impersonation (e.g., someone makes a fake account of them)
- Repeatedly contacted by someone they do not want to be contacted by
- Networked harassment (e.g., a group of people organized online attacks against them)
- Experienced harassment online because of their gender, race, sexual orientation, disability, gender expression or other marginalizing factors (gendered harassment)

Transgender and gender-diverse people reported the highest proportion of incidents experienced, with cis women reporting slightly higher proportions of incidents of online harm compared to cis men. Although men and women reported relatively similar numbers of incidents of online harm in several categories, women were much more likely to report a serious impact from online harms compared to men. LGBTQ+ people were much more likely to report a serious impact from online harms compared to heterosexual people.

A 2019 study by Deeptrace, an Amsterdam-based cybersecurity company providing deep learning and computer vision technologies for the detection and online monitoring of synthetic media, paints a stark picture: 96% of deepfakes are of an intimate or sexual nature, primarily targeting women.[10] It's nearly impossible to talk about deepfakes without bringing up pornography, which targets and harms women. The study also shows that deepfake pornography may have a disproportional impact on Asian women.

This deliberate targeting underscores the vulnerability of women to exploitation and abuse through this technology. The victims are often actresses, musicians, and media professionals, highlighting the potential for deepfakes to damage reputations and careers. In contrast, deepfakes without explicit content primarily target men, often politicians and corporate figures.

These findings underscore the risk for AI, particularly in the realm of deepfakes, to exacerbate existing inequalities and create new avenues for harm. The consequences extend beyond individual victims, impacting brand reputations, legal liabilities, and the broader ethical landscape of AI development.

The potential of AI is vast, but we must be vigilant in ensuring that this powerful technology is used responsibly and ethically. Deepfakes are a stark reminder that the future of AI is not predetermined.

The Role of AI in Employee Well-being

AI can be a powerful co-pilot in promoting employee well-being, offering data-driven insights to create a healthier and more productive workforce. The two areas AI can make an impact are *mental health support* and *improving physical health*.

Mental Health Support

AI has started to make a significant impact in *mental health support*. AI-powered chatbots can provide confidential and readily available mental health support, offering resources, coping mechanisms, and even initial assessments for common mental health concerns. These chatbots aim to fill the gap in the shortage of human therapists and provide 24/7 support to individuals in need.

Woebot, a chatbot developed by Alison Darcy, is a rules-based AI system that uses a database of research from medical literature, user experience, and other sources to provide support to users. It is designed to bond with users and keep them engaged, using a team of staff psychologists, medical doctors, and computer scientists to construct and refine its database. Woebot's responses are predictable and controlled, reducing the risk of providing harmful advice.

Tessa, another chatbot designed to help prevent eating disorders, uses generative AI, which can generate original responses based on information from the internet. However, this type of AI can be unpredictable and may provide harmful advice, as seen in the experience of Sharon Maxwell, who challenged the chatbot and received counterproductive advice such as lowering calorie intake and using tools like a skinfold caliper to measure body composition. The psychologist who helped lead the team that developed Tessa said that was never the content that the medical team wrote or programmed into the bot. Tessa was taken down after Sharon Maxwell's experience was reported to the National Eating Disorders Association.[11]

As we can see from these examples, AI-powered chatbots can be a valuable support tool for mental health therapy, especially in addressing the shortage of human therapists. However, GenAI systems can be unpredictable and may provide harmful advice. These chatbots must be designed with input from medical professionals and should be regularly reviewed and monitored to ensure they provide effective and safe support to users. If you are selecting AI tools to support employee mental health, be sure to have proper validation and testing before deploying it to employees.

Separately, AI systems can analyze a wide range of employee data, ranging from communication patterns, performance metrics, to wearable device data (for those who opt-in) to identify subtle signs that someone may be struggling with mental health issues. By applying advanced analytics to these digital trails, AI could detect rising stress levels, emotional distress, or other red flags before overt problems manifest. This capability opens a window for proactive early intervention and connecting employees with appropriate resources before situations escalate.

However, the decision to implement such proactive monitoring is a complex one that organizations must carefully weigh. There are serious concerns around employee privacy, consent, and data governance that legal teams will scrutinize closely. Just because the AI capabilities exist does not automatically justify their use. Organizations must have a clear strategy and process for how to appropriately handle new capabilities such as employee monitoring. If AI systems spot potential problems, but the organization lacks adequate mental health support capacity, that can create additional legal and ethical challenges.

There's also the critical question of whether employees would feel this type of AI monitoring is too invasive, even if anonymized and opt-in. If there is already low psychological safety, this proactive monitoring, while well-intended, may exacerbate mental health challenges. It'll be essential for employees to co-design and have full transparency around such systems' purpose and constraints for buy-in.

Ultimately, responsibly deploying mental health AI monitoring requires a balanced, meticulous approach—one that maximizes the potential upsides of earlier support intervention while stringently protecting employee privacy, reducing legal liabilities, and fostering an organizational culture of psychological safety and trust. Getting this calibration right is extraordinarily challenging but critical for tapping into AI's unique strengths as a force for improving workplace mental health and well-being.

Physical Health

AI can also play a role in improving physical well-being for employees. AI-based fitness trackers and apps can monitor employee activity levels, provide personalized exercise recommendations, and even offer virtual coaching sessions. This can help employees stay motivated and achieve their fitness goals. One practical application of wearables is in the trucking industry due to the high-stress nature of the job. Early intervention and support for mental health issues, identified through signs like persistent fatigue, irritability, changes in appetite or sleep patterns, social withdrawal, and feelings of hopelessness, are becoming increasingly important. Telematics and wearable technology are revolutionizing risk management and driver well-being, providing data to prevent accidents, reduce claims, and ensure driver safety.[12]

I remember working for a company that had an on-site nutritionist years ago. It was very helpful to get a personalized plan that I could easily follow. Few organizations offer such benefits today, and remote work has also made it less practical to hire nutritionists on-site. AI-based nutrition apps can analyze dietary habits, provide personalized meal plans, and offer guidance on healthy eating choices. This can help employees make informed decisions about their food choices and water intake and improve their overall health.

Achieving a healthy work-life balance is essential for both employee well-being and productivity. AI can help by optimizing work hours and ensuring that employees have sufficient time for rest. For example, AI can provide a reminder to rest based on the number of hours in back-to-back meetings. This can help prevent burnout and improve overall job satisfaction.

The Complex Picture of GenAI's Impact on Productivity

If GenAI is so powerful, shouldn't it be able to reduce employees' workload and give them more free time? Not exactly.

However, that is certainly the expectation. Recent research from Upwork, involving 2,500 global C-suite executives, full-time employees, and freelancers in the United States, United Kingdom, Australia, and Canada, reveals high expectations among executives for AI's efficiency benefits.[13] A significant 96% of C-suite leaders anticipate that AI tools will boost overall productivity. Yet, for many workers, the value proposition remains unclear, with some finding AI adds to their job challenges.

The study examines AI's impact on workforce productivity, the extent of expected AI integration, and why these implementations haven't fully realized their productivity potential. Achieving optimal productivity, efficiency, and employee satisfaction requires a fundamental rethink of work structures and evaluations. Executives face a dilemma, as 81% have increased expectations for employee output via AI (37%), skill expansion (35%), broader responsibilities (30%), office return (27%), improved efficiency (26%), and extended hours (20%).

In my own conversations with employees across industries, there is a heightened sense of anxiety around how GenAI will impact their jobs. Leaders can ease this anxiety by communicating frequently and offering more transparency around their plans to develop and upskill the workforce. Even if the plans are not completely baked, it provides more assurance to employees knowing their leaders are thinking about it. It's also critical to continue to assess internally what impact AI has had on workload and expectations to minimize frustration.

Responsible and Ethical AI Principles for Workplace Well-being

While AI offers significant potential for improving employee well-being, it's essential to be aware of the potential risks and implement proper processes to ensure responsible use. Additionally, data collection and analysis must be conducted ethically and transparently, with clear consent and safeguards in place to protect employee privacy.

To ensure that AI is used in a responsible and ethical manner, I'd recommend starting with these principles, as shown in Figure 5.1. While there are several established Responsible AI principles from large tech companies, the sensitivity of well-being data requires a different level of care. Let's explore each of the principles further.

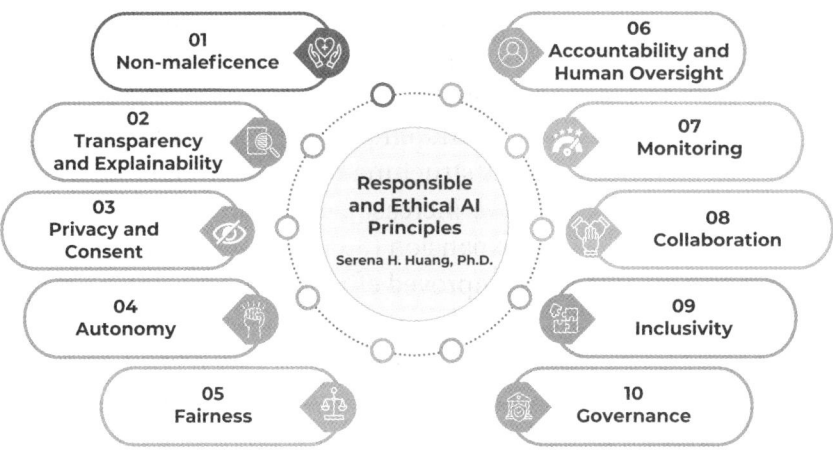

Figure 5.1 Responsible and Ethical AI Principles by Serena H. Huang, Ph.D.

- **Nonmaleficence:** Ensure that AI systems do not cause harm to employees. This principle emphasizes the importance of designing and deploying AI tools that prioritize employee safety and well-being.
- **Transparency and Explainability:** Clearly communicate to employees how AI-powered well-being tools work, what data are collected, and how that data will be used. Ensure that AI-powered well-being tools provide transparent and explainable outputs, enabling employees to understand the reasoning behind recommendations or interventions.
- **Privacy and Consent:** Implement robust safeguards to protect employee privacy, including data encryption, secure storage, and access controls. Obtain explicit consent from employees before collecting and analyzing their data.
- **Autonomy:** Prioritize employee autonomy, allowing individuals to opt-out of AI-powered well-being tools or request human support if desired.
- **Fairness:** Ensure that AI systems are designed to be fair and unbiased, avoiding perpetuation of existing inequalities.

- **Accountability and Human Oversight:** Establish clear lines of accountability for AI-powered well-being tools, including designated responsibilities and consequences for misuse. Implement human oversight and review processes to detect and correct potential biases or errors in AI decision-making.
- **Monitoring:** Regularly monitor and evaluate the effectiveness and ethics of AI-powered well-being tools, making adjustments as needed.
- **Collaboration:** Collaborate with experts in AI ethics, data privacy, and mental health to ensure that AI-powered well-being tools are developed and implemented responsibly.
- **Inclusivity:** Actively involve diverse groups of employees in the design, development, deployment, and oversight of AI systems. This ensures that the tools are equitable and considers the needs of all employees, especially those from underserved communities.
- **Governance:** Establish clear governance structures for AI systems, including policies, procedures, and oversight mechanisms to ensure compliance with ethical standards as well as global and regional regulations.

When implementing AI-powered well-being tools, whether it's a chatbot or a wearable device, following are questions to ask vendors during the initial conversations.

Data Privacy and Governance

- What types of employee data will be collected and used to train or run the AI system?
- How will employee consent be obtained for data collection and use?
- What data governance policies and technical safeguards will be implemented to protect employee privacy?
- How will the collected data be secured, who will have access, and how long will it be retained?
- How can individual organizations and employees request a copy of their data or purge their data completely?

Fairness and Bias Mitigation

- How will the AI models be audited for potential biases and discriminatory outcomes?
- What procedures will identify and mitigate unfair biases toward protected groups?
- Beyond "do no harm," what processes and controls will be in place to ensure beneficial outcomes across all demographics?
- How will input from the AI governance council in our organization be incorporated?
- What levels of human oversight will exist over the AI system's outputs and recommendations?
- How will human reviewers be trained to identify potential errors or risks?
- Will our employees be able to opt-out and request human-led well-being support in real-time if requested?
- How will users report potential biases and harmful output from the AI system?

For internal alignment, these are additional questions to discuss with your stakeholders within the company.

Transparency and Explainability

- How will we communicate to employees how the AI system works and what data are being used?
- How will we collaborate with the vendor to ensure the AI system provides output and recommendations in understandable ways?
- What internal processes do we need to stand up for employees to request further information or raise concerns?
- What resources and additional team members will we need to ensure employees' concerns and questions are properly handled?
- What change management strategies will we implement to ensure the adoption of AI across the organization?
- How will we train employees to effectively use and interact with the AI system before and during the implementation?
- What ongoing support and training resources will be available to employees post-implementation?

- How will we keep employees informed about the progress and updates related to the AI system?
- How will we communicate the successes and benefits of the AI system to maintain engagement and support?

Ethical Principles and Accountability

- How do the AI system's design and intended use align with our ethical values and responsible AI principles?
- What external AI experts and mental or physical health experts' guidance will be incorporated?
- What accountability measures do we need to put in place if issues occur?
- What contingency plans are in place to address any unforeseen challenges?
- How will the impact on employee well-being be measured, reported, and continuously monitored?
- What potential risks have been identified in the deployment of the AI system, and how will we mitigate them?
- What processes will be in place for regular review and evaluation of the AI system's performance?

Interdisciplinary Collaboration

- What is our long-term vision for the use of AI in our organization?
- What ethical guidelines will we follow to ensure responsible AI use?
- What future developments or enhancements do we anticipate for the AI system?
- How will we ensure the sustainability and scalability of the AI system?
- What specific roles will legal, privacy, security, HR, IT, and data science play in the design and deployment?
- How will we ensure that the AI system complies with all relevant legal and regulatory requirements?
- How will we address any ethical dilemmas or conflicts that arise during the AI system's deployment?

- How will our employee perspectives be continuously incorporated into the AI system's evolution?
- How will we collaborate with peers in other companies for knowledge-sharing purposes?

AI has the potential to transform the way we approach employee well-being, but only if we use it responsibly and ethically. By asking the right questions and having necessary conversations early on, business leaders can fully leverage the power of AI to create a work environment in which all employees thrive.

"AI Makes Assumptions!"

In one of my implementations of an AI recruiting tool that ranked candidates, we discovered a strange phenomenon during the testing process.

You see, this AI software was marketed as a way to not only speed up resume screening, but also improve diversity by removing unconscious biases that human reviewers can inadvertently bring. A key selling point was that the AI would evaluate candidates impartially based solely on skills, experience, and job fit.

However, we noticed a concerning pattern emerged during the testing process. Candidates who most resembled the profile and demographics of our existing leadership team were consistently scoring higher than others. On the surface, this seemed logical—of course, current executives were "successful hires." But without explicitly telling it to do so, the AI made the assumption that replicating the same hiring decisions of the past was the ideal path forward.

In essence, the tool was inadvertently reinforcing the lack of diversity we had been working to improve. Rather than offering a fresh, impartial perspective, it was simply mirroring and perpetuating our historical disadvantages when it came to recruiting underrepresented candidates.

(continued)

(continued)

We also uncovered another issue around the AI's ability to evaluate resumes for certain functions that tend to have high volumes of Asian candidates. The system frequently struggled to understand names and determine gender from these applicant pools. Initially, one of our goals was to use the AI to help identify where candidates from different backgrounds were falling out of our hiring funnel so we could reinforce those leaks. But with such flawed data, we knew enabling that feature would lead to bad information and poor decision-making.

Clearly, this tool was not ready for primetime use within our organization. The test findings were disappointing in some ways, as we had high hopes for using AI to remove human bias from hiring. However, I'm grateful we were rigorous in our testing because these issues would have gone undiscovered until likely too late.

This experience reinforced a critical learning: we cannot take vendor promises at face value without scrutinizing how tools actually perform in the real world.

Bias, flaws, and misalignments with your specific company goals can still happen. Organizations must pair AI rollouts with comprehensive testing processes to make sure they are used for good, rather than just do no harm.

Human-centered AI to Eliminate Bias

A 2023 article emphasizes the importance of human-centered AI (HCAI), which involves collaborating with humans from diverse backgrounds throughout the entire process of designing, developing, and implementing AI systems.[14] The goal is to ensure that AI operates transparently and delivers equitable outcomes that benefit people and society.

Here's a summary of the key roles and how they contribute to HCAI in the healthcare setting:

- Human-centered design specialists ensure AI systems are usable, accessible, and meet user needs.
- Ethicists, social scientists, and lawyers advise on ethical, social, and legal implications.
- Healthcare workers provide input on design and ensure AI aligns with patient/provider needs.
- Healthcare managers evaluate the appropriateness, risks, and fairness of AI implementations.
- AI/machine language practitioners develop the AI systems with a human-centered mindset.
- AI education specialists communicate AI's capabilities and limitations and promote responsible use.
- Communication scientists bridge technical and human aspects of AI development/deployment.
- Patients and communities provide feedback to meet their needs and avoid unintended consequences.

Human-centered Versus Traditional AI

Traditional AI emphasizes task automation for efficiency, while HCAI prioritizes human needs, values, and capabilities. In contrast to traditional AI, HCAI aims to augment human capabilities rather than replace them. This design philosophy prioritizes understanding and respecting human needs to ensure that AI systems are accessible, user-friendly, and ethically aligned.

In HCAI, teams actively involve users in the design process to create solutions finely tuned to real-world needs. HCAI systems adapt and learn from human behaviors and are context-aware.

Several examples illustrate the differences between HCAI and traditional AI:

- **Personalized learning systems:** In education, traditional AI might focus on the automation of grading or generic educational content. HCAI, in contrast, creates adaptive learning platforms that adjust content and teaching styles to fit individual student's learning patterns, preferences, and needs. This approach enhances the learning experience and outcomes, adapting to human behaviors and preferences.

- **Healthcare applications:** Traditional AI might focus on maximizing efficiency in data processing and diagnostic procedures. HCAI, on the other hand, may not only assist in diagnosis but also consider patient comfort, privacy, and emotional well-being. For example, AI tools in mental health are designed to provide therapy and support in a manner that is sensitive to and respectful of the patient's psychological state.

- **Customer service:** Traditional AI deploys chatbots and automated systems that focus solely on efficiency. HCAI, however, designs these systems to understand and respond to human emotions, providing a more empathetic and personalized customer experience. These AI systems can detect customer frustration or confusion, adapt their responses accordingly, or even escalate to a human operator when necessary.

- **Smart home devices:** Traditional AI might focus on automation and control of home devices. HCAI, in contrast, designs smart home systems that learn from and adapt to the residents' routines and preferences. It creates an environment that is not only efficient but also comfortable and conducive to the well-being of its inhabitants.

Applying to Well-being at Work

Defining the group of experts is key. Experts who are healthcare professionals will be needed on the team. For instance, mental healthcare professionals can help evaluate and test the AI solution proposed to improve employees' mental well-being. Nutritionists can evaluate the meal plans and nutrition advice provided in the tool. Data scientists can help with making sure the algorithm is doing what it's intending to do and recommending safeguards. HR experts can help evaluate the impact the solution will have on the overall talent strategy. For transparency, it is helpful to include some employees in the design process as well. Ultimately, every well-being technology will likely need a slightly different set of experts and stakeholders to ensure it's human-centered.

The GenAI Journey

Responsible AI (RAI) has been part of every AI conversation I've heard recently. If your organization is just getting started, consider taking a look at existing frameworks rather than starting from scratch. Organizations including Microsoft, IBM, and National Institute of Standards and Technology have all published guidelines.

When Microsoft HR started its GenAI journey, it leaned into the company's Responsible AI Standard—encompassing the principles of accountability, inclusiveness, reliability and safety, fairness, transparency, and privacy and security.[15] The plan of application of AI for HR is pinned onto the functional business architecture, which is pinned onto the RAI standard.

HR professionals were also key to the creation of AI-powered bots to interact with employees on both routine and more complex topics, deployed through channels including Microsoft Teams. Empowering HR professionals to drive AI allowed HR employees to envision AI's potential impact in an "experiential way" rather than through a top-down narrative. Because of their involvement in the company's AI journey, HR team members became more comfortable with the technology, enabling broad deployment of tools like its Copilot across HR. Microsoft rolled out the GenAI-powered tool in Dynamics 365 Customer Service and Microsoft 365 for its HR Service Centers and in Microsoft 365 for the entire HR organization, driving both productivity improvements and increases in job satisfaction.[16]

Beyond the Framework: People and Process

After standing up data ethics councils in F500, I've learned that the RAI framework isn't useful without identifying the **right people** and **creating a sustainable process**. You cannot govern AI without governing the data. After speaking with chief data officers

(CDOs) about AI governance, it's clear that there are lots of different approaches today. One common theme is there's a council or committee of some sort that is cross-functional.

People: The Heart of AI Governance

What level should the council and committee members be? C-level? Vice president? Director? Manager?

- **C-level:** CEO, CDO, CIO, CHRO, CTO, CFO, or other top executives who can drive organizational change and allocate resources
- **Vice President and Director:** Leaders with expertise in AI, data science, ethics, and compliance, who can provide strategic guidance and oversight
- **Manager:** Subject matter experts who can operationalize AI governance and ensure day-to-day compliance

The ideal composition will vary depending on the organization's size, industry, and AI maturity. A company in a highly regulated industry may require a different mix, for instance. More importantly, the responsibility of council members must be clearly defined. At minimum there should be representatives from technology/IT, security, Data and Analytics Center of Excellence (COE), legal, privacy, labor and employment, compliance, as well as people analytics. Most successful councils I've seen do not necessarily have every functional leader at the same level. It may seem counterintuitive. It is "simple" to have every representative be of the same level, but it is unrealistic in practice for them to have the appropriate capacity and expertise for the council.

Process: The Backbone of AI Governance

A well-defined process is critical to the success of the AI governance council. Here's a suggested framework, illustrated in Figure 5.2:

- **Intake:** Establish a clear process for submitting any AI projects or initiatives that would use employee data, including data collection, use cases, and potential risks.

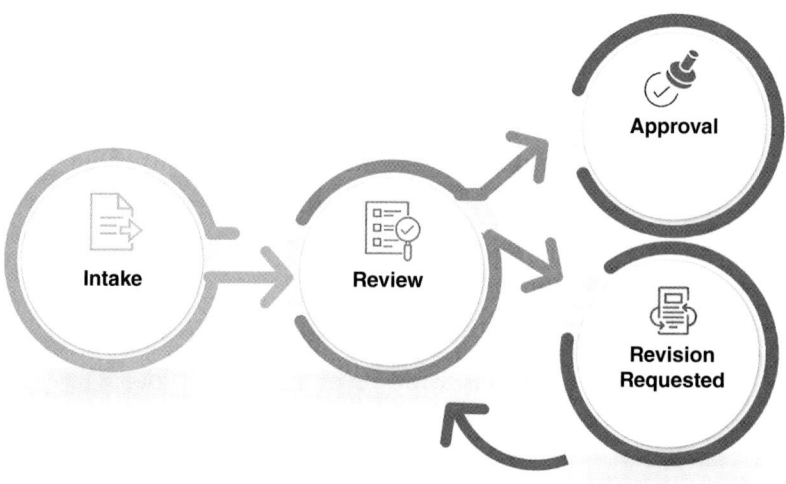

Figure 5.2   AI Governance Council Process by Serena H. Huang, Ph.D.

- **Review:** The council reviews submissions, assessing the risks versus benefits and compliance with organizational policies and regulatory requirements.
- **Approval or Revision:** The council approves or requests for a revision on AI projects, providing guidance on mitigating risks and ensuring responsible AI development.

Additionally, when the council is formed initially, the members should do the following:

- **Establish policies and procedures:** Develop and maintain guidelines for AI development, deployment, and monitoring. Again, you can start with the existing public frameworks.
- **Offer training and education:** Partnering with the appropriate teams internally ensure employees understand AI and data ethics, risks, and compliance requirements.
- **Conduct ongoing audits and assessments:** Monitor AI systems and projects to ensure ongoing compliance and identify areas for improvement.

Decide whether or not to have an automated approval and rejection process and whether there is a regular meeting where requestors get to pitch their use case. You can also determine whether an appeal process is allowed. If this sounds overwhelming, I've been able to create an automated process where the requests are automatically approved if an initial assessment is passed. I collaborated with everyone on the council to design an assessment that goes through a series of questions around data gathering and usage. If the answer is no to every question on the assessment, then it's automatically approved, with a copy of the details going to everyone on the council as well as the requestor. This ended up saving a lot of time and provided a way for requestors to think through how the data would be used.

If you are looking for frameworks that focus more on risk management, the National Institute of Standards and Technology AI Risk Management Framework (AI RMF) is a great resource. It provides AI organizations with a guiding structure to operate within and outcomes to aspire toward, all connected to their specific contexts, use cases, and skillsets. The rights-affirming framework operationalizes trustworthy AI within a culture of responsible AI practice and use.

What's an AI system? **The AI RMF refers to an AI system as an engineered or machine-based system that can, for a given set of objectives, generate outputs such as predictions, recommendations, or decisions influencing real or virtual environments.** AI systems are designed to operate with varying levels of autonomy. Think about this description in the context of HR for a moment. Would the job application system in your organization be an AI system because of the automatic rejection of candidates? Would the internal marketplace that recommends current employees who are a good fit for open roles be an AI system? Would the compensation tool that recommends pay increases be an AI system?

The Future of AI-driven Inclusion and Well-being

The future of AI-driven inclusion and well-being lies not in replacing human judgment and interaction but in augmenting them. AI should be seen as a tool that enhances human capabilities, not as a replacement for them. This means fostering a collaborative approach where AI systems act as partners, providing data-driven insights, automating tasks, and identifying patterns that humans might miss.

How should your organization approach AI-human collaboration? Keeping in mind the principles mentioned earlier in this chapter, there are a few ways you can use the strengths from AI and humans to improve the inclusion and well-being of employees:

- **Data analytics augmentation:** AI can analyze quantitative and qualitative data to identify patterns that might be invisible to humans or human analysts who are not experts in diagnostic analytics. This information can then be used to inform human decision-making, leading to more informed and equitable outcomes. For example, AI can analyze employee data to identify inequality and other issues in employee experience, allowing HR professionals to adjust their strategies for greater fairness.
- **Support customization:** AI can customize and personalize support for employees, ranging from recommendations for mental health resources, training opportunities, or career development based on individual needs and previous feedback. Of course, human interaction remains crucial for providing appropriate guidance.
- **Manual tasks elimination:** AI can automate repetitive tasks, freeing up managers and HR professionals to focus on more strategic work. This can include tasks like scheduling meetings, managing emails, or generating monthly reports, allowing them to dedicate more time to building relationships and encouraging innovation.
- **Oversight provision:** Humans must remain at the center of AI development, testing, and deployment, ensuring ethical guidelines are followed and biases are mitigated. This involves careful monitoring of output from AI systems, continuous evaluation of their impact on employees' health and well-being, and a willingness to quickly adjust or intervene when issues arise.

By leveraging human-AI collaboration, we can envision a future of work where AI is used responsibly to create a more inclusive and well-being-focused workplace for all employees. We must not forget the potential risks of AI so there are two key considerations to keep in mind.

- **Ethical considerations:** To use AI responsibly, especially on well-being and inclusion aspects for employees, leaders must prioritize ethical considerations. Establishing an internal council with guidelines for AI systems, ensuring employee data privacy, and maintaining transparency are crucial steps in building trust within the organization. As healthcare costs continue to rise, some technology vendors prioritize cost minimization as a criteria in recommendations, and this is an example of ethical issues to align on for organizations contemplating AI system implementations.
- **Continuous listening and adaptation:** Since AI technologies will continue to evolve, organizations must listen for feedback continuously during and after implementation. This can inform a strategy change or address issues timely. Leaders can also benefit from adopting a culture of continuous learning to ensure that everyone remains informed about the latest AI advancements. As with any technology that moves and changes quickly, staying flexible and adaptable will be key to successful implementation.

The recent advancements in AI present a unique opportunity for organizations to redefine the future of work. By leveraging AI responsibly, leaders can create an environment that not only enhances productivity but also enriches the human experience for all employees. As we wrap up this chapter, here are some reflection questions to ponder:

1. How can AI be integrated into our current workflows to enhance *both* productivity and employee well-being?
2. What is the biggest pain point where we haven't considered AI as a solution but should?
3. How can we cultivate a culture that embraces continuous learning in the age of AI?

The future of work lies in creating a workplace culture that prioritizes inclusion and supports the overall well-being of employees. The intersection of data, AI, and post-pandemic talent strategies offers a unique opportunity to redefine how we work. In the final chapter of this book, we will explore how to be "human-first" and thrive in the future of work.

Notes

1. Bertrand, M. and Sendhil, M. (2004). Are Emily and Greg more employable than Lakisha and Jamal? A field experiment on labor market discrimination. *American Economic Review* 94(4), pp. 991–1013.

2. Gerdeman, D. (2020). Minorities who "Whiten" job resumes get more interviews—recruiting. Harvard Business School. Available at: https://www.hbs.edu/recruiting/insights-and-advice/blog/post/minorities-who-whiten-job-resumes-get-more-interviews

3. Smith, G. and Rustagi, I. (2022). Workplace AI wants to help you belong. *Stanford Social Innovation Review.* https://doi.org/10.48558/AA2S-PD93

4. Cross, R., Oakes, K., and Cross, C. (2021). Cultivating an inclusive culture through personal networks. *MIT Sloan Management Review.* https://sloanreview.mit.edu/article/cultivating-an-inclusive-culture-through-personalnetworks/

5. Cecchi-Dimeglio, P. (2017). How gender bias corrupts performance reviews, and what to do about it. *Harvard Business Review.* Available at: https://hbr.org/2017/04/how-gender-bias-corrupts-performance-reviews-and-what-to-do-about-it

6. Jampol, L., Rattan, A., and Wolf, E.B. (2023). Women get "nicer" feedback—and it holds them back. *Harvard Business Review.* Available at: https://hbr.org/2023/01/women-get-nicer-feedback-and-it-holds-them-back

7. Myers, A. (2023). *AI-detectors biased against non-native English writers.* Stanford HAI. Available at: https://hai.stanford.edu/news/ai-detectors-biased-against-non-native-english-writers

8. IBM. (2024). *Data suggests growth in enterprise adoption of AI is due to widespread deployment by early adopters.* IBM Newsroom. Available at: https://newsroom.ibm.com/2024-01-10-Data-Suggests-Growth-in-Enterprise-Adoption-of-AI-is-Due-to-Widespread-Deployment-by-Early-Adopters

9. Elhussein, G., Hakspiel, J., and World Economic Forum. (2024). *Classroom to C-suite: Getting more women in STEM careers.* Available at: https://www.weforum.org/agenda/2024/03/empowering-women-in-stem-how-we-break-barriers-from-classroom-to-c-suite/

10. Adee, S. (2019). *World's first deepfake audit counts videos and tools on the open web* [online]. IEEE Spectrum. Available at: https://spectrum.ieee.org/the-worlds-first-audit-of-deepfake-videos-and-tools-on-the-open-web

11. LaPook, J. (2024). Mental health chatbots powered by artificial intelligence developed as a therapy support tool. *CBS News* [online]. Available at: https://www.cbsnews.com/news/mental-health-chatbots-powered-by-artificial-intelligence-providing-support-60-minutes-transcript/

12. Davis, C. (2024). *Metrics, mental health and multimillion settlements.* Available at: https://www.insurancebusinessmag.com/us/news/workers-comp/metrics-mental-health-and-multimillion-settlements-497813.aspx

13. Upwork. (2024). *From burnout to balance: AI-enhanced work models for the future.* Available at: https://www.upwork.com/research/ai-enhanced-work-models

14. Chen, Y., Clayton, E.W., Novak, L.L., Anders, S., and Malin, B. (2023). Human-centered design to address biases in artificial intelligence. *Journal of Medical Internet Research.* doi: https://doi.org/10.2196/43251

15. Microsoft. (2024). *Responsible AI principles from Microsoft.* Available at: https://www.microsoft.com/en-us/ai/responsible-ai

16. Colletta, J. (2024). *3 key learnings from Microsoft's journey to adopt AI in HR.* Available at: https://hrexecutive.com/3-key-learnings-from-microsofts-journey-to-adopt-ai-in-hr/

Chapter 6
The Future of Work: Human-first

The future of work is data-informed and AI-powered. Let's remember to put human first, always.

– Dr. Serena Huang

We have been talking about "the future of work" for years, and then the COVID-19 pandemic accelerated remote work overnight. We went from commuting daily to working from home five days a week. The multi-year debate we have been having around return-to-office (RTO) made me wonder if we have truly made progress. Then I remembered: People don't like change or change that is *done to them*.

Leaders did not like how COVID-19 shut down the world and forced everyone to work from home. There was a sense of "return-to-normal" many likely desired. Employees have been vocal about needing flexibility in the post-pandemic world and made headlines when they said no to promotions in exchange for working from home, for instance.

At the core of these debates isn't "flexibility," but rather "autonomy" and "trust." We don't want flexibility—what we want is that our employer trusts us and shows us that they trust us by giving us autonomy to work in a flexible way.

A 2023 *Harvard Business Review* article highlights the connection between employee well-being and having a sense of autonomy: "Ditching the commute allowed people to lighten their financial load, gain back time in their day, and better control their mental and physical health. Gartner research has found that autonomy not only reduces workers' fatigue by 1.9 times, it also makes them 2.3 times more likely to stay with the organization. Leaders are now grappling with how to facilitate their organization's transition back to more in-office work, particularly in the face of our research which found 67% of employees feel that going to the office requires more effort than it did pre-pandemic and 60% of employees say the cost of going to the office outweighs the benefits."[1]

There appears to be some generational difference. While all employees value connections with their colleagues, Gen Z employees are most likely to say they would go into the office to build relationships with their managers and colleagues.[2] Leaders must be more intentional about helping their teams build the connections that can lead to both personal and professional growth, including mentorship, sponsorship, coaching, and other project opportunities.

In the RTO debate, everyone knows there is a difficult trade-off between flexibility with connection. Many hybrid employees have also had an underwhelming RTO experience: they go to the office to connect with colleagues, only to find it empty, and they're left zooming from the office or doing work alone that they could have done at home.[3] Coming out of the pandemic, many organizations opted to mandate a minimum number of days per week, but employees who followed this model didn't show higher performance, according to the Gartner data.[4]

The organizations I've spoken to that take a more contemporary approach focusing on employee autonomy and connection create off-sites where teams gather outside the office on a regular basis, instead of mandating days per week or month. A change in environment can also provide a boost to creativity and innovation.

Strategic Workforce Planning

Planning out the future has become more and more complex. Traditionally, companies only needed to figure out how many people to hire. Now, there are part-time employees, temporary workers, interns, independent contractors, and, of course, bots. How will they work together, and what skills should be possessed by each of these types of workers? The equation suddenly becomes complicated.

Strategic workforce planning (SWP) is about preparing the organization for future talent needs. It involves understanding the skills required to meet long-term business objectives and ensuring that the workforce is equipped to deliver on these demands. Traditionally, organizations have had to wait for competency models to be built and survey or assess employees to have detailed data on employees for planning purposes. It doesn't need to be the case anymore with technology advancements. AI can significantly enhance SWP by providing near real-time data on employees' skills based on their experience and project work, predicting talent needs, and identifying skill gaps. Once the gaps are identified, AI can even help organizations create tailored learning programs for each employee based on their skills and career goals.

Having implemented workforce planning technology in large organizations, I'd suggest having in-house expertise on the topic. While most vendors and implementation partners can provide consulting support, they would not have the business context for your organization. Properly translating business forecasts into headcount needs, for instance, will often a deep understanding of how your business operates.

While AI increases the ease of implementing SWP, there is also now an urgent need for organizations to figure out (1) *how AI will impact the jobs employees currently hold*, and (2) *how to prepare the organization to work effectively with AI*. A recent LinkedIn study estimates that *55% of jobs will be changed, either augmented or disrupted*. Your employees are likely wondering what this means for their job security and career progression. It's critical to start communicating how the leadership is thinking about reskilling and to listen to employees during these times of change.

For those of you in organizations with SWP capabilities, have you revised the workforce plan at your organization since ChatGPT came on the scene like a storm? Whether you use a workforce planning software or a homegrown spreadsheet, there are a few questions to ponder if you want to future-proof your workforce strategy.

1. Which segment of the workforce will see improvements in productivity from GenAI?

To answer this question, you can break down the segments into roles and then roles into skills and tasks. Let's take nursing roles as an example. Is a nurse always doing work that can only completed by a nurse? Providence Health System used a simple and brilliant framework to solve the talent challenge for its 52 hospitals, 950 clinics across 25,000 physicians, 35,000 nurses, and 120,000 caregivers. Their Chief People Officer asks a powerful question, "What parts of each role can be done differently to increase the joy of practice, add capacity, or improve the quality, cost, or experience of care?" This is not meant to replace the jobs of any nurse entirely, but to find ways to take away the dull and dangerous part of their jobs.

> When Providence deconstructed their nursing roles down to the task level, they found that 30–40% of the tasks could be done by others—whether administrators who were previously nurses or doctors, or other staff with minimal training doing tasks such as taking temperatures, check-ins on stable patients, etc. Some tasks could also be automated, such as scheduling and some documentation.[5]

You can apply the same methodology to the roles in any organization, and I'd recommend starting with the roles with *the highest impact on the future revenue* rather than trying to boil the ocean. Large companies like GE and IBM have long been using skills data in workforce planning. Instead of asking employees to document their skills and their manager to validate these skills, which can be extremely time-consuming, you can use skills tech platforms that leverage AI to infer skills based on employees' job history and project completion data.

2. Will the organization see fewer low performers? Can Performance-improvement plans be accelerated?

In the Harvard Business School and Boston Consulting Group study, lower performers see a 43% gain in their performance from using GenAI, while high performers see a 17% gain.[6]

There is so much potential for organizations to be more proactive in the performance management space. Imagine if you can improve the performance of your bottom 10% or 20% in the short term. How will this impact the organization's business performance? Could performance-improvement plans be accelerated or even eliminated completely?

3. How will employee engagement and attrition evolve in the short and long term?

There is undoubtedly both excitement and fear when it comes to GenAI. Randstad's 2023 survey finds that the majority (52%) believe that AI will improve their career and promotion prospects, far outstripping fears of using the technology. However, there is a gap in training and development, since a mere 13% of employees have been offered any AI training, while 33% of employees already using AI within their day-to-day roles. Will the lack of training on GenAI erode employee engagement and increase attrition risk? It's a possibility given the importance of learning and development to most employees. The 2024 PWC survey shows more than 1 in 10 workers who have not used GenAI at work say their employer does not allow the use of GenAI tools, and nearly a quarter say their employer hasn't given them access to GenAI. Do you know how your employees across different segments feel about GenAI and their expectations for your organization to provide development opportunities?

While resignations have slowed down, the employees' intent to leave jobs remains high. A recent PWC survey concludes that employees are restless, with 28% of respondents saying they are likely to change jobs in the next 12 months (up from 26% in 2023). To put in context, the same survey found 19% of employees say they're likely to change employers in the next 12 months during the "great resignation" of 2022. Interestingly, the survey suggests job satisfaction has ticked up slightly from last year: 60% of employees say they're very or moderately satisfied, compared with 56% who said so last year. Given these seemingly contradictory data points, it is more important than ever to not rely on a single metric such as employee engagement once a year to understand employee sentiment. In addition to pulsing regularly, it would be helpful to conduct stay interviews for retention purposes.

Key Skills for the Future Workforce

The World Economic Forum's Future of Jobs Report 2023 estimates a quarter of jobs (23%) are expected to change in the next five years, with 69 million new jobs created and 83 million eliminated.[7] There is particular concern about developing the skills for the so-called "jobs of tomorrow," such as those needed for the digital, green, and energy transitions. While a "skills-first" approach potentially holds the power to transform the labor market,[8] the "Race to Reskill" was a major part of the discussions at Davos 2024, the Annual Meeting of the World Economic Forum in Switzerland.[9]

A separate discussion around human skills has been gaining attention in the age of AI. While AI continues to advance at a rapid pace, certain human qualities remain very difficult to replace. These qualities will continue to remain essential for effective leadership as well as interpersonal relationships in and outside the workplace. Figure 6.1 summarizes the seven critical human skills in the age of AI.

Emotional Intelligence

Emotional intelligence (EQ), the ability to recognize and manage emotions effectively, is a critical human skill. Unlike AI, which processes information based on algorithms and data, humans can draw upon their personal experiences, relationships, and emotions to interpret and respond to situations.

7 HUMAN SKILLS

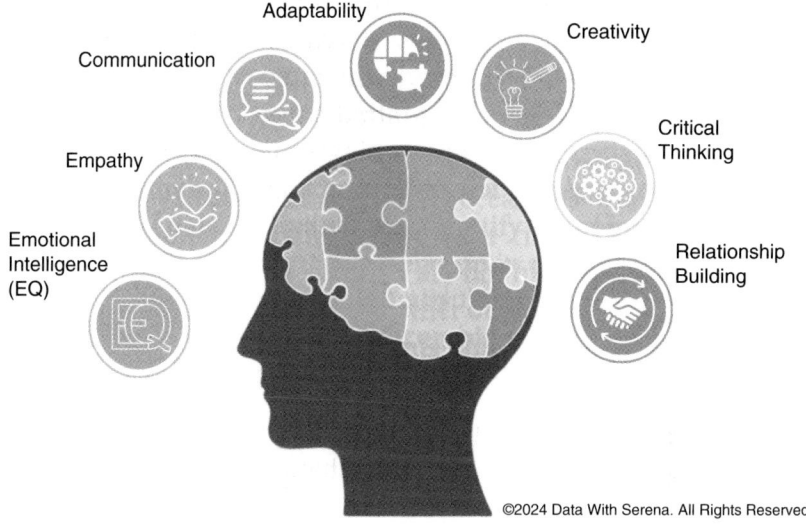

Adaptability

Creativity

Communication

Critical
Thinking

Empathy

Emotional
Intelligence
(EQ)

Relationship
Building

©2024 Data With Serena. All Rights Reserved.

Figure 6.1 Seven Human Skills by Serena H. Huang, Ph.D.

To enhance EQ, it's important to cultivate self-awareness, manage stress, and develop empathy for others. By understanding our own emotions and the emotions of those around us, we can navigate complex social situations with greater effectiveness. In addition to taking online training about EQ, you can also try journaling to better understand and process your own emotions regularly. Separately, going to therapy can be a great way to improve your understanding of triggers and how to regulate your emotions.

For school-age children, it is a positive sign that many schools have started to teach them how to identify and express their emotions at an early age. These EQ curriculum can help them grow into young adults who can recognize and manage emotions effectively.

Empathy

Empathy, the ability to understand and share the feelings of others, is a distinctly human trait that transcends the capabilities of current AI. Human empathy involves a complex interplay of nonverbal cues, verbal language, tone of voice, cultural nuances, and intuitive understanding.

Note that EQ and empathy are related but not the same. Empathy allows you to tune into how someone else is feeling, but EQ provides the broader framework to then regulate your own emotions, maintain self-control, and build connections through skilled interactions. High EQ requires empathy, but also incorporates additional competencies for applying emotional awareness.

Can AI understand our feelings? While facial recognition technology has made significant strides, it still falls short in accurately interpreting subtle micro-expressions and the underlying context. Additionally, biases make it difficult for facial recognition technology to accurately understand the expressions of certain demographic groups.

Empathetic managers and leaders are better able to understand and appreciate the unique perspectives, experiences, and challenges faced by employees from diverse backgrounds. This understanding can help them create a more inclusive environment where employees feel valued and supported. Empathetic managers are more attuned to the emotional needs of their employees. They can identify signs of stress or burnout and provide appropriate resources, which contributes to overall employee well-being.

Communication

Effective communication involves more than just exchanging information. It requires active listening and understanding nonverbal cues, which are difficult for AI at the moment.

Cultural differences, idioms, sarcasm, and indirect implications are difficult for machines to interpret accurately. Additionally, communication often involves creative expression, storytelling, humor, and improvisation. AI lacks the imaginative spark and spontaneity that humans bring to creative communication. However, AI can process and generate language, which can certainly enhance our communication to some extent.

It is a bit counterintuitive to say GenAI cannot communicate like a human can; many people first used ChatGPT to help draft emails or write essays for their homework. GenAI can generate language and even act as a great translator, but we must not forget that the ability to understand deeper context and nuance is still uniquely human. In the workplace, effective communication from managers helps motivate, empower, and inspire employees.

Adaptability

The pandemic and the post-COVID recovery have challenged our ability to stay resilient and adaptable. Adaptability is the ability to adjust to changing circumstances, priorities, and deadlines. While AI can process vast amounts of data and recognize patterns, it lacks the ability to adapt to unexpected situations or think on its feet. Top leaders understand that adaptability is more than reacting to change, but also being able to anticipate and drive change. They are comfortable with not having all the answers and saying they don't know. This requires a high degree of emotional intelligence, self-awareness, and humility, all of which are human skills.

To develop adaptability, it's important to embrace a growth mindset. Individuals who believe their talents can be developed and improved have a growth mindset. On the other hand, those with a fixed mindset believe they were born with a set of talents and abilities that cannot improve or change. We shall cultivate a curiosity for learning and being open to feedback to stay adaptable in the era of AI.

Creativity

Creativity, the ability to generate new concepts and solutions, is a human trait that AI struggles to replicate. It is true that AI can generate art or music based on large amounts of data or past patterns, but it lacks the ability to think outside the box and provide truly original ideas. We humans, on the other hand, have the capacity for imagination and intuition, which are essential for driving innovation.

To nurture creativity, it's important to engage in activities that inspire us regularly. This may include traveling or taking up new hobbies. Effective leaders understand that creativity is about creating a culture that encourages experimentation, risk-taking, and learning from failure. They are not afraid to challenge existing assumptions and conventional wisdom.

Critical Thinking

Critical thinking is the ability to analyze and evaluate information, arguments, and assumptions. While AI can process vast amounts of data and recognize patterns faster than we can, it cannot think critically and make complex human judgments. Human leaders, on the other hand, have the capacity for critical thinking, which is essential for making informed decisions, solving complex problems, and evaluating risks and opportunities.

Effective leaders understand that critical thinking is not just about analyzing data, but also about considering multiple perspectives, evaluating evidence, and making informed judgments. They are able to separate fact from fiction and are not afraid to challenge assumptions and conventional wisdom. This requires a high degree of cognitive ability, analytical thinking, and social skills, all of which are uniquely human.

In the world full of fake news and misinformation, critical thinking is more important than ever.

Relationship Building

Relationship building is the ability to establish and keep connections with others, which requires understanding human emotions, language, and behaviors. It is true that AI can use pattern recognition to identify our emotions to some degree, but AI can't build relationships in the same way people can. In rare cases, we have heard of marriages between humans and AI or the rise in popularity of AI boyfriends or girlfriends. The bond between AI and people won't be like it has been portrayed in sci-fi movies, with people and robots living alongside one another 24–7 and developing romantic or family-like relationships.

Besides effective communication and emotional connection, successful relationship building also requires finding shared values or common ground and being able to maintain trust with each other. These are all unique human skills.

AI cannot fully replicate the unique qualities that make humans special. By developing and nurturing our human skills, we can complement the capabilities of AI and create a more fulfilling future together. Leaders and managers can consider shifting workforce strategy to focus on hiring and developing these human skills to be prepared for the future.

Organizations of the Future: Human-first Cultures

At an organizational level, leaders and teams must also adapt to AI and focus on creating a "human-first" culture where employees feel valued, seen, heard, supported, and empowered to thrive.

To start, we need to recognize that the traditional leadership style focusing on "command-and-control" ignores the human needs of our employees and will not be effective in the rapidly changing work environment.

Leaders and managers must continue to learn new skills and evolve toward being much more empathetic, adaptable, and inclusive. This may require a fundamental shift in priorities for many organizations.

The findings from the interviews I've conducted for this book are clear: successful organizations treat DEI and well-being like any other business initiative. These organizations do not treat these initiatives as HR programs or feel-good measures. They know that constant emotional tax for employees who don't feel included is too high for the organization.

One of the silver linings of the COVID-19 pandemic is that mental health is less of a taboo topic in the workplace. In fact, it's becoming a key differentiator for organizations looking to attract and retain top talent. The 2024 Deloitte Global Gen Z and Millennial Survey shows that younger employees expect their employers to do more to prioritize their well-being. Only around half (52% of Gen Zs and 54% of millennials) feel confident that their manager would know how to help them if they did raise these concerns, and nearly 3 in 10 believe that their manager would discriminate against them if they were to raise concerns about mental health (27% of Gen Zs and millennials).[10]

Leaders of the future must prioritize creating a culture that supports well-being, encourages open dialogues, and provides resources for employees to manage stress and anxiety. This means being proactive about creating a safe and supportive environment rather than just reacting to mental health issues when they become emergencies.

Inclusion is also critical in creating a human-first culture. This means fostering an environment where everyone feels seen and valued to contribute. Leaders must recognize and address any potential biases, encourage and reward diverse perspectives, and ensure that every team member has a sense of belonging. The research is clear: there is a strong connection between belonging and engagement. When employees feel like they belong, they are more likely to be engaged and committed to staying with the organization.

How can leaders foster this sense of belonging? One key strategy is to prioritize psychological safety. When employees feel safe, they're more likely to take risks, share ideas, and collaborate with others. Leaders can create this sense of safety by encouraging open and honest communication, embracing vulnerability and imperfection, and fostering a growth mindset. Another strategy is to infuse inclusion and well-being across the employee life cycle from hire to exit. It starts with the hiring process, where leaders can prioritize DEI by using AI-powered tools to reduce bias and ensure that job descriptions are inclusive. Once employees are hired, leaders can remind them about their access to well-being programs, such as mental health resources, employee assistance programs, and flexible work arrangements.

We can't talk about well-being and inclusion without discussing flexible work arrangements. More than four years since the start of the pandemic, are we still getting it wrong?

In August 2024, Eric Schmidt, former Google CEO, got serious backlash for claiming remote work hurt Google's innovation in the AI race. It is true that many remote employees crave a sense of connection through in-person interactions, but employees are now looking to their leadership team to make the commute "worth their effort."

As employees progress in their careers, leaders can continue to prioritize their well-being by providing opportunities for growth and development, recognizing and rewarding their contributions. The connection between providing career growth opportunities and well-being is clear. In large organizations I've interviewed, transparency about an employee's potential in the organization can greatly ease their anxiety about their future and improve retention. This can be achieved through regular career conversations and letting high-potential employees know where they stand. For DEI programs that focus on career development and growth, this level of transparency is particularly important.

Inclusion goes beyond these big moments like promotions and hiring. Lexy Martin and Melissa Arronte explain in their research that there are multiple events and places where leaders can demonstrate to employees that they are valued.[11]

Martin and Arronte define inclusion as the extent to which employees can reach their full potential to contribute and make a difference. This is consistent with how Organizational Network Analysis (ONA) can quantify inclusion, as we discussed in earlier chapters. Meeting invites, chats, and slack participation are all signals for the level of inclusion at different events and places, or "moments."

Their **inclusion experience framework** defines five inclusion moments:

- **Decision Moments:** Places where decisions are made that impact outcomes, such as growing revenue and new product innovation. These decisions are made in strategy, planning, budget, and key talent discussions.

- **Process Moments:** Organizational events associated with attracting, hiring, developing, promoting, and retaining talent.
- **Network Participation Moments:** Places where communication, information, and decisions flow through an organization formally (meetings) or informally (events).
- **Personal Moments:** Interactions employees have with the organization, their manager, their teammates, and policies that they perceive as fair and reflecting inclusive treatment or not.
- **Culture Moments:** Culture behaviors are the ways that organizational culture plays out between bosses and employees, teammates, and task assignments reflecting inclusion.

HR Process Changes to Enable Change

Creating a human-first culture requires more than just a shift in leadership priorities. It also requires a fundamental transformation of the way we approach HR and talent development. HR plays a critical role in creating incentives to align and reward managers for these new skills. This can include training and development programs that focus on EQ, empathy, and inclusion, as well as performance metrics that prioritize employee well-being and engagement.

Realign Incentives and Rewards

To reinforce a human-first culture and new leadership behaviors, HR must ensure that incentives and rewards are aligned with the organization's new priorities. This may involve the following:

- **Recognizing and rewarding contributions to employee well-being and inclusion:** Celebrating managers and employees who demonstrate empathy and other human-first skills. Create new key performance indicators to evaluate manager's performance based on their effectiveness in promoting a healthy and inclusive workplace.

- **Offering flexible work arrangements:** We have learned from the pandemic there is no one-size-fits-all policy that works anymore. HR can partner with senior leaders to create new policies that support employees' work-life balance and well-being by providing the flexibility needed.
- **Investing in professional development:** Provide opportunities for employees to develop their skills to future-proof their careers, including opportunities related to mental health, inclusion, and new leadership behaviors.

Invest and Transform Learning and Development

Learning and development programs must be redesigned to focus on the behaviors, skills, and competencies that are essential for success in a human-first culture. This may include the following:

- **EQ training:** Helping employees develop their ability to understand and manage emotions effectively. Prioritizing the development of additional skills such as empathy, active listening, conflict resolution, and communication.
- **Trauma-informed workshops:** Educating managers and employees to become trauma-informed. Since the pandemic, we know trauma has and will continue to impact many of our colleagues in different ways. Increasing our understanding and response to trauma will create a happier and healthier workplace. Specifically, it helps us understand why someone might be reacting in a way that doesn't make sense to us. This awareness further allows us to adjust our own behaviors so we don't risk re-traumatizing our colleagues.
- **Human-first leadership training:** Equipping leaders with the skills they need to create a supportive and inclusive workplace. Measuring the effectiveness of this training will also be important for long-term success.

Transform HR to Become Human-centered and Data-informed

I can imagine this might ruffle some feathers to claim HR needs to be human-centered. However, traditional HR practices often prioritize efficiency and cost-effectiveness, sometimes at the expense of true employee well-being. To foster a human-first culture, progressive CHROs must shift their focus to creating an environment where employees feel valued, seen, and empowered:

- **Prioritize well-being and inclusion for holistic employee experience:** Investing in programs and initiatives that support employees' mental and physical health. Offering flexible work arrangements and supporting employees in managing their personal and professional responsibilities.
- **Promote transparency in talent management:** Providing transparency in where employees stand in the organization is critical for well-being and retention. Employees also pay close attention to who gets promoted to see if any new leadership behavior requirements are lip service. If the organization has a "no jerks" rule, do jerks continue to stay or even get more opportunities? For changes to last, HR needs to reward managers who demonstrate new leadership skills and create a positive workplace culture.
- **Redesign performance management:** HR must create new performance management systems that align with organizational priorities, including developing performance metrics that measure inclusive leadership behaviors and employee well-being.
- **Require every HR professional to leverage data in decision-making:** HR has so much data at its disposal, yet much of it has gone unused or underutilized in decision-making. With advancements in GenAI and widely available education, business leaders will continue to expect their Human Resources Business Partners (HRBPs) to bring more and more data to talent-related discussions and decisions.

The future of work is about creating a workplace culture that is more human and more supportive of employees' overall well-being. The convergence of data, AI, and post-pandemic talent strategy presents an unprecedented opportunity to reshape the very essence of how we work and how we support the individuals who drive our organizations forward. By using data and AI-powered strategies, leaders can create a workplace culture that prioritizes the well-being and inclusion of all employees, and that fosters a sense of community and connection.

Notes

1. Shells, K. and Duffy, C. (2023). Return-to-office plans don't have to undermine employee autonomy. *Harvard Business Review.* Available at: `https://hbr.org/2023/11/return-to-office-plans-dont-have-to-undermine-employee-autonomy`

2. Gartner. (2023). *Gartner HR survey finds 77% of employees are placing increased importance on manager support.* Available at: `https://www.gartner.com/en/newsroom/press-releases/2023-06-22-gartner-hr-survey-finds-77-percent-of-employees-are-placing-increased-importance-on-manager-support`

3. Gartner. (n.d.). *Hybrid workforce.* Available at: `https://www.gartner.com/en/human-resources/insights/managing-hybrid-workforce`

4. Gartner. (2023). *Gartner HR survey reveals less than half of employees are achieving optimal performance.* Available at: `https://www.gartner.com/en/newsroom/press-releases/05-23-2023-gartner-hr-survey-reveals-less-than-half-of-employees-are-achieving-optimal-performance`

5. Institute for Corporate Productivity. (2024). *Building the workforce of the future—by deconstructing the work.* Available at: `https://www.i4cp.com/meetings/i4cp-2023-next-practices-weekly-march-2-2023` [Accessed 3 Nov. 2024].

6. Dell'Acqua, F., McFowland III, E., Mollick, E., et al. (2023). Navigating the jagged technological frontier: Field experimental evidence of the effects of AI on knowledge worker productivity and quality. *Harvard Business School Working Paper 24-013.*

7. World Economic Forum. (2023). *Future of jobs report 2023: Up to a quarter of jobs expected to change in next five years.* Available at: `https://www.weforum.org/press/2023/04/future-of-jobs-report-2023-up-to-a-quarter-of-jobs-expected-to-change-in-next-five-years/`

8. Moritz, R.E., Zahidi, S., and World Economic Forum. (2023). *How a skills-first approach can help people get better jobs.* World Economic Forum. Available at: `https://www.weforum.org/agenda/2023/05/adopting-a-skills-first-approach-help-people-better-jobs/` [Accessed 3 Nov. 2024].

9. World Economic Forum. (2024). *The race to reskill.* Available at: `https://www.weforum.org/events/world-economic-forum-annual-meeting-2024/sessions/the-race-to-reskill` [Accessed 3 Nov. 2024].

10. Deloitte. (2024). *The Deloitte Global 2024 Gen Z and Millennial Survey.* Available at: `https://www.deloitte.com/global/en/issues/work/content/genz-millennialsurvey.html`

11. HRM Asia. (2022). *Moments that matter in the inclusion experience.* Available at: `https://hrmasia.com/moments-that-matter-in-the-inclusion-experience/`

Index

Note: Page numbers in **bold** refer to figures and tables.